Teaching a Chicken To Swim

Edited by Rob Middlehurst

seren

seren is the book imprint of
Poetry Wales Press Ltd
Nolton Street, Bridgend, CF31 3BN, Wales

www.seren-books.com

© the contributors, 2000

ISBN 1-85411-291-0

A CIP record for this title is available from
the British Library

*The publisher works with the financial assistance of the
Arts Council of Wales*

This book is supported by the University of Glamorgan

Printed in Plantin by CPD Wales, Ebbw Vale

Contents

Foreword

For many years, art colleges have held their degree shows, and music colleges their showcase concerts. Here the public can encounter, perhaps for the first time, the work that has been going on in the privacy of studio and rehearsal room. Already there will be a buzz about certain students. Some will already have sold a painting, given a recital, or had a composition performed.

Creative writing courses are now beginning to exhibit their graduates' writing with the same verve. In the public mind, there is now less mystery about what a creative writing course entails, and more understanding that just as a violinist needs years to build technique, so a writer cannot be satisfied with gift and impulse. After months of drafting and criticism, after the impassioned, tough, detailed workshop discussions, after the tutorials, e-mails and phone calls, the work has got to go into the outside world on its own, and make its way without special pleading.

The writing in this anthology requires no special pleading. Much of it has already found a publisher, and several of these names are already making a stir in the review columns. The University of Glamorgan is immensely proud of its Masters in Writing graduates, and with reason. These students are dedicated to reaching their potential as writers. They make extraordinary efforts and sacrifices in order to do so. One student flew in from the USA for her residential weekends; others have come from Ireland, Italy and the Balearics. Most students have to reorganise their jobs, home life and finances. Their commitment to their own writing and to that of their fellow-students is impressive. The network of support and friendship which develops between each cohort of students and their tutors is correspondingly strong, and lasts well beyond the course itself.

I taught on creative writing courses at the University of Glamorgan for eight years, and on the Masters degree course for the first five years after its inception. Graduates of these courses have become good friends. I read their novels as they come out, go to their launches and public readings, catch their plays on the radio, and read their poems in magazines or in collections. Already the harvest is beginning, and some of the first-fruits are collected in this anthology.

No creative writing degree can plant the seed of talent in a writer, but a good course nurtures that talent, challenges it, and develops it confidently as the writer's technique matures. A conversation begins between the evolving writer and his or her contemporaries, which will continue throughout that writer's working life. Such conversations have been at the centre of the Masters in Writing at Glamorgan. Now the voices of these gifted, exciting writers are ready to speak directly to their readers, off the page.

Helen Dunmore

Introduction

The nineteen writers in this anthology are all former students of the Masters in Writing at the University of Glamorgan. As the Biographical Notes show, many of these writers have achieved considerable success since they completed our Masters courses: in having novels or collections of poetry / short stories published; in winning or being shortlisted for literary prizes – e.g. Barbara Bentley, Amanda Dalton, Pamela Johnson, Mo McAuley, Julie Rainsbury, Dan Rhodes, Sarah Salway, Victor Tapner. Richard Evans' first novel *Entertainment* has recently been published, and Maria McCann's *As Meat Loves Salt* is due in 2001. Many have had their work published in magazines and anthologies; some have been awarded bursaries by Arts organizations – for example Lynne Rees, Euron Griffith. All are active writers; several are also using their skills as literary editors or part-time teachers of creative writing.

Since 1993 when the Masters in Writing was started, nearly 40 students from Britain, Ireland and several other countries have completed our two-year distance learning course. Each student has a tutor who comments on drafts in regular postal, e-mail and telephone critiques; students also attend short residential courses at the University.

In compiling *Teaching a Chicken to Swim*, I have only considered work by our Masters students up to 1999. This cut-off point made the selection a little easier. As I discovered, editing has been a painful pleasure: a combination of celebration and exclusion. There was plenty to celebrate in my opening paragraph. At the end of this section, let me apologise to all the former students who were left out, this time.

The selection of work was collaborative. In most cases the writers themselves helped me choose by stating their preferences; more often than not I was spoilt for choice. In a few cases, my ever-helpful colleagues at Glamorgan, especially Christopher Meredith and Sheenagh Pugh, recommended poems or stories. And when I needed the anthology title, a telephone conversation with Lynne Rees about her poems gave me just what I was looking for.

And what was I looking for in the writers' work? Examples of poems and prose fiction which represented each writer's distinctive qualities, in terms of: use of language (image, rhythms, form, an ear for dialogue), engrossing narrative voice and perspective; an individual take on specific themes, characters, settings; and above all that special power to capture something authentic (an experience, a thought, a dream, a place, an object) in a way that stays with you and makes you return to the piece again and again.

The themes and approaches in these poems and stories are too diverse to discuss adequately here, so I will limit myself to a few points and a brief comment on each writer. Overall, I was struck by the writers' intense interest in language, character, relationships and memory.

In some of the poetry, memories of people figure strongly against a variety of domestic and natural backgrounds, for example: Frank Dullaghan's short sequence of portraits of Daddy in *Frames;* Julie Rainsbury's sensual evocations of people, real and imagined, in familiar and exotic settings; Malcolm Lewis's concentrated perspective on past lives and activities embedded in *Settee;* Fiona Owen's graphic recollections of family scenes in various locations. In *Out of the Blue,* Amanda Dalton combines narrative and haunting imagery to explore the boundaries between memories and dreams. Barbara Bentley's work exploits the dramatic tensions of idiosyncratic voice and imagery within controlled forms. In her vivid poems, Lynne Rees captures not just observed experience but the feel of people and things; some of Victor Tapner's spare and powerful poems explore the continuing presence of our ancestors from early history.

The stories adopt a variety of approaches and range across time and place. Maria McCann's intriguing novel extract shows a group of characters in the English Civil War; in Richard Evans's *Time,* the narrator, in the here-and-now of his south Wales flat, speculates on time travel. There are stories about childhood: Caryl Ward takes us back in time to a girl's experience of school in south Wales; Mo McAuley's Sorting Out the Ponies focuses on the real and imaginative life of a little girl in the North West of England when mangles were still in use.

Some of the writers portray characters and relationships in public and private places. Edward Boyne's *Intifada* is an economical story about the narrator's relationship with an American journalist in London and riot-torn Bethlehem. Robert Doyle's work is represented by two novel extracts: the narrator of *The Pervert* recounts a disturbing sexual experience; in contrast, *Bert and the Bees* (an extract from *God's Boxer*) captures the bizarre and spicy dialogues between the characters as the scene changes from steak house to council house. Pamela Johnson's *Wig Night* is a subtle and engaging monologue in which the life and character of the narrator is gradually revealed as she discusses her trade secrets and the private needs of her customers. Sarah Salway's compelling story, *Leading the Dance,* reveals the sly expressions of threat and power from husband to wife at a school ceilidh.

And there's humour: from the sharp, subversive parody of Euron Griffith's themepark to Dan Rhodes's witty, miniature stories on girlfriends, romantic love and disappointments. Paul Lenehan's two stories can be savoured for their humour, the idiosyncratic insights into character, the wonderful rhythms of the prose.

Time for thanks. Firstly, thanks to all nineteen writers for their interest in this anthology and for our telephone tutorials (my most distant one with Ed Boyne, when I disturbed him on his mobile in a bookshop in Galway).

Thanks to all the Masters in Writing tutors for contributing in so many ways to the success of these writers. To the full-time University tutors: Tony Curtis (Director of the Masters in Writing), Matthew Francis, Christopher Meredith, Sheenagh Pugh. To our hard-working and illustrious part-time tutors, past and present: Gillian Clarke, Helen Dunmore,

James Friel, Sian James, Stephen Knight, Catherine Merriman.

Thanks to the Research Committee in the School of Humanities & Social Sciences at the University of Glamorgan for supporting this project.

Thanks to Shelagh.

Rob Middlehurst, September 2000

Barbara Bentley

Rock-a-Bye

'You were in a long time, and visiting
was weekends only. We didn't have a car.
It was three buses and an uphill walk
to get to you. We never missed. Your mother
always cried when we got back.

And it was strict. There was a nurse
who poured scalding tea down your throat
so you almost choked. Course, you were
strapped down, so you couldn't fight back.
But you spat. And your mother wept.

Two years it was. Uncle Bill was kindness itself.
He had a car so he picked you up
and took you through the Illuminations.
But you were sick down your mother's coat
And you howled for that wretched nurse.

You couldn't use a knife and fork.
If a door banged shut, you jumped.
Horses. Cats. Dogs. You screamed at them all.
But trees were the worst. You sobbed
your heart out, that day at the park.

I'm told this story repeatedly, as if
in the telling I'll latch on to the child
just as she was – in a pram, in the park
full of strangers and beasts
and monster oaks wired with lights.

But she's lost like the nameless baby
in a cradle-song: the one who fell
from the windtorn boughs.
Her ghost still haunts the babbling leaves
as if she were real, once upon a time.

Mother's Nightmare

Her child is running past fields
where policemen in waxed coats are raking
the undergrowth, then down by the lake
where they'd fed the ducks, but this time
the frogmen are diving deep, hooking trainers
and bits of inner tube.
                    Cut to the meeting
with the press, where she is over-exposed
and cameras flash red dots in her eyes
and she can taste mascara in her mouth
as she pleads for witnesses.
                    Then back to her child
who has stopped by the site where a digger
scoops earth, and in the films there's always
a white hand poking through silt like
unwanted crockery, but the child
turns the corner and skips down their lane
where the cherries are weeping and sniffer dogs
chained to each gate pick up her scent
and pant in the heat.
                    Over to the station
where travellers are pigeons flapping
this way and that, past a child's face
that's stuck on the pane at *Information*,
but a fibre-tipped moustache is daubed
on the glass, over her mouth, and nobody
sees the joke.

Hurry back to her child
who has reached their front door and is
captured on pause. Just look at her socks
rucked at her ankles, her bus-pass face
and that ballpoint heart stretched on her hand
as she turns the handle, turns the handle.

Across the Ice

We were on the ice together.
I picked the flakes from your lashes,
greased your lips, gave you names to distinguish
the long-necked birds in the sky,
the plump birds on the shores,
the big fish and the little fish
that sparked the waters around us.

And you shouted the words, so loud
that your voice came back
as whalesong. Day after day,
wave after wave. When the sun was up,
your hands mimed wings,
their shadows beating
something or nothing on white.

You craved food and warmth,
so I wrapped you in the skin
of caribou; we shared its flesh
in the long dark, when wolf-noise
harpooned the space
between a flicker of light
and sleep. We were dreaming

every morning would be the same –
yesterday's kerosene still in the air,
a glossary of names to learn,

that pearl horizons repeat.
But something shifted.
Your blood on the ice steamed
redder than anything newly dead

and a crack opened up, so the rink
where we lived was split –
you on that side, me on this.
I watched you drift to the outpost
where tractors thrash the ice.
Perhaps you remember hand-stitched furs
and some of the words for snow.

Botched Job

You mixed prozac with booze, and you drank it
like pop. Then you swayed to the pub
where everyone guessed you were pissed.
At the leper's seat by the fruit machines
you downed one more pint – warm froth
on your lips – while *Eve of Destruction*
blared from the juke box, three decades late.
The boys in the backroom pocketed balls
in a greengold haze. Dominoes clacked
from the tap. Maybe you caught the chat-ups
on bar stools, the bell, the call
for last orders, though nobody budged

and dreams fizzled out into Rizla dust
as your roll-up burnt on the Tetley's rim.
It was always the same. You'd seen rockets
light up the Disney turrets while you wished
upon stars that were light years away;
you'd clocked in and out of the ICI works
where the waste of weeks went up in smoke

and fell to earth as synthetic flakes.
No home to go to? the barman said.
Perhaps you swore and kicked up a fuss
since the cops drove you back. You slumped
in a chair in your room where you'd painted
bare branches on every wall. A dog barked
somewhere inside them, somewhere far off,
and you strained to hear that wilderness howl,
but it got less and less, what with the hills
and the trees and the polymer blizzards,
the great dunes of toxics blocking the roads.

Edward Boyne

Intifada

Our car slowed to a crawl behind an Israeli army jeep. Soldiers held black rifles pointing upward towards the steel coloured sky.

We passed the 'Holy Manger Stores', its special offers on mincemeat, pitta bread and olives, scrawled in Arabic on plate glass. There were groups of young Arab men, sour looking in leather jackets. Some women find them sexy. They all look the same to me, the same black moustache, that reliably dark look around the eyes.

We parked near the huge police station in Manger Square which was ringed by racks of razor wire. The wire clustered in dense webs of clean sharpness.

The car park fumed with giant coaches. Small boys sold peanuts, silver coloured canned sugar drinks, cellophane wrapped umbrellas, faded postcards by the half dozen. A man at a kebab stall roasted lamb on a black spit over a charcoal fire. Men in brown raincoats circled the coach doors offering themselves, in short conspiratorial breaths through blackened teeth, as guides to the sacred site of the nativity.

'I will show you everything, all the history, the whole history.'

A Jewish boy on the police station steps in green fatigues cradled a Galil automatic and gazed at us. He held a lighted cigarette to his mouth. His breath in the cold air plumed in different thicknesses of air and smoke.

We stood by the car for the short moments needed to button or unbutton coats, to take an umbrella, to sniff the air for food smells, unspecified dangers.

'Lot of people,' said Mitch, tightening his blue scarf.

'Christmas season starting early,' I said. I meant it as a joke. It was early October.

I saw his eyes move quickly and warily over the scene.

There were far more people than I expected and not so many tourists. A lot of locals, all hanging around, not doing much. In the few days since he arrived he had learned the necessary caution, the necessary attention to movement and signs. I hadn't expected him to learn so quickly.

'Car should be safe here,' said Mitch, checking that the doors were locked. I had borrowed the car from Kurt, one of the men from the kibbutz.

'As safe as anywhere I suppose,' I said.

We approached the church. I could feel raindrops on the crown of my head.

Mitch said: 'Why don't we get a guide for once?'

'A guide? Why do you need a guide to visit a church? Anyway, I've been here before several times.'

I felt irritated. I wanted to be all the guide that he needed.

'It's not just any church and you know that,' he said. 'I'm a bit vague on the history of the place, that's all. I don't know who built it or when it was built. You miss out on all the subtleties. Anyway I'm sure a guide wouldn't cost much.'

'It's ridiculous Mitch. We don't need a guide for a small place like this. What I've read about it will come back to me, don't worry.' I squeezed his hand. The first time I'd touched him for years. His hand was fleshy cold.

The door to the church reminded me of a trapdoor in a wall. Mitch had to bend down.

Inside the building the smell of wood preservative from the floor boards and the roof beams thickened the air. I could feel my throat tighten and corrugate. What light there was came mainly from oil lamps hanging from the ceiling and from candles flickering in large candelabras.

An official looking sign near the door outlawed bare heads, leggy skirts, shorts, flesh of all kinds. Priest figures in black floor length robes moved quietly like shadows on the shadows. I whispered to Mitch that different Christian sects laid claim to the church and stalked each other warily inside its precincts.

'I don't know all the details,' I said.

'Hello I'm Lucy from Alabama, are you with the Blue Line group?'

'Sorry, no,' said Mitch.

There was a life-size Jesus doll set in crumpled kitchen tinfoil. It was in front of an altar on what was intended as a manger. The doll, the manger and the altar were surrounded by bullet proof glass.

'So this is the spot where it all happened,' said Mitch.

'Yes, it must be,' I said.

'My daughter used to play with dolls like that,' said Mitch. 'It was in the days before political correctness.'

'It is a bit gross, I suppose.' I wasn't sure what else to say.

A middle-aged woman in a black mantilla headscarf knelt down in front of the manger. She started to chant a prayer in Latin. Two other women in black joined her, their blackstockinged knees pressed passionately against the ancient wood. A tall priest with tiny veins reddened on his cheeks paused behind the three of them. He carried a silver incense holder. He gave the women the sign of the cross with one hand, releasing incense in a sideways motion with the other.

Mitch couldn't control a cough. The naked doll was lying with its feet perched up on straw and the three women were chanting in Latin, their eyes downcast.

'Is this it?' he said in a tone of mock surprise.

'There's more downstairs. Have you heard of the Holy Innocents? They're the children murdered by Herod when he was trying to kill the baby Jesus. Herod has had a bad press from Christians since.'

I can be mocking too. I just wanted him to know.

We moved down the narrow staircase carefully, holding onto the metal railings. At the bottom of the stairs was a glass case filled with bones and skulls. There was a kneeling area in front with a weeping nun in full black habit. She could have been atoning for Herod's sins, for the loss of the children two thousand years before, or for something more immediate. I wasn't tempted to ask.

'Those bones should be buried,' said Mitch. 'They must have belonged to someone. They're the bones of real people. Who knows when they died. It could have been recently.'

'Don't you believe the story?' I said. 'The story about

Herod and the children? It's supposed to be fact.'

'You're not seriously saying that these are the bones of children murdered by Herod's soldiers?'

'People believe it,' I said, staring further into the glass case as if an ancient child might appear to bear testimony.

'There's no harm in belief. It doesn't hurt anybody. I think you've got to believe. What have you got if you haven't got belief?'

Without answering Mitch moved further into the basement. Huge wrought iron candelabras with dozens of blazing candles hung from the ceiling. Night lights, votive offerings, shone out of various grottoes and side altars. Each flame twisted and shivered in the secret draughts from under doors, down stairwells and hidden passages. He stood for several minutes at the far end of the huge room. He might have been a shadow on the wall. I felt like he was staring in my direction but he was too far away for me to be sure.

Eventually I saw him turn and walk back to the stairway. He pressed his way firmly up past tentative tourists, back into the main body of the church.

I came up a few minutes later.

'What happened to you?' I said. 'I looked around and you were gone. Didn't you like it down there?'

I knew I sounded irritated again.

'I'd had enough,' said Mitch. 'It's your average medieval church basement. They have better ones in Italy. Anyway, I needed to get some air. Why don't we head off somewhere else?'

'I thought you wanted to get more about the history of the place.'

I could feel my anger rise. I had wanted more from him, more than this scepticism. I didn't know exactly what I wanted, maybe to see him impressed or touched by something.

'The mood has gone off me,' he said. 'Let's go and get some coffee.'

As we walked towards the door, I noticed that a group had gathered there, just inside the entrance. They looked anxious.

I sensed from them through the half dark, the slow throb of alarm.

Mitch hadn't noticed but was pointing to Roman mosaics on the floor.

'There must have been a big Roman building on this site originally,' he said. 'In Herod's time perhaps. It's a pity more of it hasn't survived.'

'Too many wars,' I said, watching the group of anxious tourists near the door. 'Nothing much has lasted for long here.'

As we approached the door a sallow skinned priest in a black hat and robes stepped out from a dark alcove.

'You must not try to leave yet. It is dangerous. The police station, many stones, petrol bombs, big crowd, maybe shooting.'

There were shouts outside, dull thuds, stacatto cracks like whips. I recoiled from the priest, instinctively grabbing Mitch's arm, my anger dissolving suddenly.

★

Sixteen years before he knew that I wanted him. We were in his car outside my parent's redbrick house in North London. I could see the upstairs bedroom curtains parting.

'Will you come and live with me in San Francisco?'

He was so direct about it I couldn't speak. I knew he had been planning to go back to America. He hated England. I had been putting it all out of my mind.

The silence went on and on. He didn't say anything, didn't try to persuade me, didn't repeat the question. With Mitch there were never any frills. I'd learned there was no way you could read something into what he said. If Mitch meant marriage he would have said marriage. 'Will you come and live with me!' No statement of future intentions, nothing more concrete than a suggestion about changing living arrangements! Hard enough for my family having to accept a gentile – but without marriage?

I could see the outline of my father against the drawn curtains. My father was a Rabbi but he was never very strict with me. Mitch was the only boy I slept with as a teenager and up to age twenty-one. I kept myself for him.

'I can't answer you right now, I need time to think.'

'That's a no,' he said. 'A no when most of you wants to say yes. There are no dress rehearsals Sarah.'

There was nothing I could say. How do you explain the obvious?

A horrible overweight black cat jumped up onto my parent's garden wall, its eyes like tiny fires in the streetlight.

The next I heard from Mitch was two years later. He was working as a trainee journalist in San Francisco. He wrote me a long letter.

The years drifted on. I didn't meet anyone special. I remember the day I got the letter about the birth of his daughter. I couldn't breathe properly for a few minutes.

> Angie and I have had a baby girl. I never thought this
> would happen to me.

Of course I wrote back. I wished them well. I told him to be sure to keep in touch.

*

I took a leave year from my job to work in Israel teaching English. The kibbutz was thirty miles north of Jerusalem. I taught Russian teenagers and children. They didn't understand the strange world they'd landed into. I explained to them that, in Israel, events which may or may not have taken place two or three thousand years ago are more important for some people than anything in the present – a country with more than its share of the god intoxicated, impatient with the world of the present and with the merely human. But there are others I told them. Not all of us are the same.

I knew he'd come some day. He wrote to me, he said that he'd always wanted to visit Israel and that his editor was interested in an in-depth treatment. Nothing about looking forward to seeing me after so long. He did mention that he was no longer living with Angie.

The day before he was due to arrive I felt tired, the sort of tiredness where you feel your blood is turning to lead. By evening I had one of my headaches.

He looked drawn but wiry, every bit the liberal west coast journalist in his pale linen jacket and crumpled silk tie. The jacket was short at the wrists. He always had long arms. He was just the same.

We shook hands. It was by far the easiest of the available options. One of the first things he said was:

'How's the teaching going?' I thought I detected a smirk. I didn't know exactly how to respond. The airport Tannoy announced a departure to Harare.

The first few days were tense. His force field had thickened and he laughed at less. I noticed again his way of asking matter of fact questions as if from a long distance, and observing, always observing. I had arranged a room for him in a vacant house just inside the compound. I could tell that the older people living in the kibbutz were suspicious of him.

*

Glass shards were spread over the car park paving stones as if a flurry of fresh hail had landed on black ice. Three tour buses were smouldering. Strings of black smoke trailed from the wire skeletons of upholstered seats. The boy sentry on the police station steps had been replaced by older, stockier men with grey helmets and visors, blue flak jackets that deepened their chests.

I felt the slide of loose glass under my soles. Patches of paving stone were stained a clotted red where young boys had been shot while throwing bricks at bullets. The bricks lay scattered where they fell, like temporary monuments.

We thought the car would be damaged if not destroyed. Instead it was gone. There was no glass or loose stones where it had been, just a flat concrete absence. We stood solemnly inside the bordered rectangle of the vacant parking place for several moments as if to invoke the car's return.

I noticed the Arab traders and church guides returning. They had the air of people practised in the recovery of atmospheres. They brushed stones and glass, set up tables with souvenirs and postcards, restored by degrees the delicate balance of commerce, religion and war.

The long wait, while cut off in the cold church, had left me feeling numb and tired. I could feel myself draw on reserves of strength like forcing sap upwards out of roots. I almost wanted to go back into the church where the tour-bus tourists and pilgrims were waiting in groups with coloured badges, watched over by competing priests. I had talked to some of them while the fighting raged outside and Mitch was nowhere to be found. He later told me he had found a vantage point to watch the riot.

We reluctantly approached the police station intending to report the missing car. Mitch wondered if the army had taken it away because of its Jerusalem number plates. I could feel my shoulders and chest tighten as we approached their warmed up rifles.

'No, we haven't taken your car.'

'No, we don't know where it could be.'

'The Bethlehem road into Jerusalem will close indefinitely at midnight. That's all. You must go now.'

In the police-station hallway we could hear metallic sounds from distant rooms and voices pitched at the higher registers of pain and panic. Mitch said he wanted to find a way to stay in the building, to record the aftermath of battle, who was to be tortured, who was to be threatened into informing. I wanted to leave straight away. I could see no reason for hanging around all those nervous looking soldiers.

He said there was a pre-ordained sequence where the details of retribution were sorted afresh, renewed and executed. Nothing was left to chance. Homes of rioters would be bulldozed or demolished by explosives, the debris flattened down. I thought this sounded a bit extreme but didn't say anything in case I might offend him. Somewhere in the distance I heard the ritual tannoy scream of a mosque starting the evening call for prayer.

Mitch sat on a bench inside the station door beside two Arab men. He started to scribble notes in rapid shorthand. One man had a small cut on his forehead which he was dabbing with a ragged piece of white cloth. With each dab a tiny half-moon of red appeared on the cloth. Both men spoke in whispers and signs. They glanced warily at Mitch who I reckon was silently attempting to tune into their frequency.

I stood near the door uncertain where to place myself. I felt I had landed in a zone where anything was possible, where the usual rules and ideals did not apply. Everything depended on what you could represent, what you stood for in the subtle shades between the politically exempt and the disposable. I wanted to say to Mitch to sit or stand somewhere away from the Arab men, not to put himself in even more danger, not to make it seem like they were talking to him.

Before I could speak a soldier in green khaki pushed in through the door. A film of sweat silvered his forehead and cheeks. His tunic had darkened under his armpits and a sweat stain was spreading across his back.

He stopped suddenly when he saw Mitch.

'No, no journalists.' He lunged forward trying to grab the notebook from Mitch's hand. Mitch instinctively pulled away. The Arab men froze in an attitude of elaborate innocence. The soldier grabbed Mitch's shirt collar and pointed the muzzle of his machine-gun at his cheek. He yelled in Hebrew in a hard military voice. A policeman emerged from an inner office with pistol drawn. Mitch had dropped the notebook on the ash-strewn floor and had put his hands up in a half-hearted gesture of appeasement.

'I am an American journalist,' he said, 'I have a press card.'

I couldn't believe what I was hearing.

'No, we are tourists, pilgrims,' I said. 'We came for the church. Our car has been stolen.'

Mitch gestured to me to be silent. The soldiers looked at me quizzically.

'She's just with me, she's not involved,' he said.

'No journalists in this place,' the officer said.

They pushed him against the wall into the search position. They patted his body down to the ankles. One of them searched the pockets of his jacket. They found his passport.

'American? Why are you here?'

He pointed to the press pass inside the folds of his passport.

I knew we'd be detained no matter what I said. We were brought into an interrogation room and searched. There was a smell of stale tobacco smoke everywhere. The officer ran his hands over me, squeezed my left breast and smirked.

'I am a Jewish woman,' I said.

He withdrew his hand immediately and without meeting my eyes, picked up my British passport from the desk and began examining it closely.

The rhythmic sound of broken glass being swept outside the station window reminded me of the sea.

I saw them confiscate Mitch's notebook and dictaphone. They put us into separate cells. I was let go after about an hour. I suppose they were in touch with the kibbutz.

They held Mitch for a lot longer. I tried to get the kibbutz people to help but there was nothing anyone could do. I couldn't see any point in trying to push it with them.

I was teaching a class when he returned to the kibbutz. He collected his bags and left me a note:

Dear Sarah,
I've decided to go to the border area with Lebanon to get another angle on things for the article. I don't think it's safe for tourists. Maybe I'll see you on my way back.
Mitch

I knew he wouldn't come back. The car was never found either. Afterwards, teaching the Russian teenagers I spoke about the modern western gentiles, their unbelief, how they doubt and humiliate their own God and how we mustn't get like that.

Amanda Dalton

How to Disappear

First rehearse the easy things.
Lose your words in a high wind,
walk in the dark on an unlit road,
observe how other people mislay keys,
their diaries, new umbrellas.
See what it takes to go unnoticed
in a crowded room. Tell lies:
I love you. I'll be back in half an hour.
I'm fine.

Then childish things.
Stand very still behind a tree,
become a cowboy, say you've died,
climb into wardrobes, breathe on a mirror
until there's no one there, and practise magic,
tricks with smoke and fire –
a flick of the wrist and the victim's lost
his watch, his wife, his ten pound note. Perfect it.
Hold your breath a little longer every time.

The hardest things.
Eat less, much less, and take a vow of silence.
Learn the point of vanishing, the moment
embers turn to ash, the sun falls down,
the sudden white-out comes.
And when it comes again – it will –
just walk at it, walk into it, and walk,
until you know that you're no longer
anywhere.

Out of the Blue

She remembered gulls at night
were floating stars on the dark sea
and shattered windscreen was blossom
that fell silently, dissolving in your palm.

She remembered what an expert she had been
at lying in bed pretending to have died;
(the barbed wire fear at the base of her spine,
the hardly breathing) and how easily metal crumples
if you hit it hard, just so.

Out of the blue, in her dream,
she would come round the edge of the quarry
at dusk. She would run up the muddied bank
to a path that led to the edge, to a drop for miles,
and a view, a panorama of the town and sea
and sand and the flat wide field
specked with bushes and pools,
and she could never tell if this was a place
she had seen or a place she would one day see
or if this was only a dream.

She remembered her grandad puppet
tangled up on the shelf –
his neck bent so far back,
wires so hopelessly crossed,
that she had taken scissors from the sewing box
and cut him free.

She remembered the flinch in her stomach,
the desperate regret, as she saw
how his limbs wouldn't dance, how he lolled,
how she would never be able to bear him like this.

Out of the blue she saw the flash
that exploded deep in her head
and she knew that the beach she had spilled onto
was motorway, and that gulls were headlights in her
      eyes,
and that she was lying far too close to the waves
that soaked her legs and almost deafened her
so that at first she didn't hear the grandad puppet
      moaning,
didn't feel the twist of guilt in the small of her back
like metal, cold and burning, as he fought for breath,
fought to find a way out of the shoebox
where she had buried him beneath the heavy soil.

And she couldn't remember the way to say she was
      sorry
and it was far too dark to find the path
that would take her back from the beach and the wide
      flat field
to the edge of the quarry and, in any case,
she suddenly realised, she was fighting for breath
and she couldn't move her legs, she couldn't move her
      legs at all.

The Gifts

You told me that I'd landed on your doorstep
like a totally inexplicable delivery
of laminated knitting patterns,
handed you a piping hot tripe supper
and a Co-op bag of dog-eared Mills & Boons.

You said it didn't help to know
that these were gifts of love.

And ever since you've looked at me
as though I'm bearing half a sack
of build-your-own-authentic-light-up Taj Mahal kits
just for you, and always dress to meet me
in your weather-beater balaclava, cover-all protector suit
and cockroach pumps.

I'd like to talk.
I'd really like to say a word or two.

But last night when I called on you
my footsteps activated garden gnomes
with powerful beams inside their hats,
your doorbell triggered angry guard-dog sound effects,
so I went home

and sat among the old, familiar clutter
in my living room – the electric whirlpool foot spa,
Jeffrey Archer hardbacks, karaoke tape
of *Wartime Love Songs Volume 2* –
every one of them a gift from you.

From *'Room of Leaves'*

Nest

I'm building a nest in the garden
and watching my breath disappear
into splintered trees.
The sky is scratched and freezing;
birds are trapped in it.

I finger veins on damaged leaves
and put my ear to the cracked soil
but there's no pulse.

My nest will be of dead and aching things,
lined with my wedding dress,
decorated with our broken flowers.

I'll sing a marriage song behind my throat
where everything is cold and trapped.
Save me from losing my breath in the hard air,
save me from screaming like birds
and wondering how things disappear.

I'm setting up home without you,
unpacking my trousseau in a room of leaves,
singing.

Frank on the Edge

If I jumped right now,
if I opened my arms
and fell with a splash
that was louder
than the crack of my head
on the rocks,
would you forgive me?

Or if I told you
that inside my heart
there's a fish
with a two inch hook
in its mouth,
gasping like crazy
and I can't get it out,
would you understand?

See, really I'm a crab
that's wedged itself

so tight in its shell
there's nothing left to do
but light a match under me.

I used to be a jellyfish,
remember?
But I've been clouding over,
drying up.
I need to go back in.
Will you throw me?

Robert Doyle

The Pervert

(Extract from a novel)

The day after mum chucked away all my porno mags was the worst of my life. I went through school in a daze, spent an uncomfortable evening eating spaghetti and making up stories about how my day had gone, then went to bed early with a feeling that can only be described as grief. I felt empty. Sick. Life had lost its meaning. All I had left was a tiny bit of a picture of an arse that looked like it had come off the *Penthouse*. I kissed it with quivering lips as I tried in vain to have my nightly wank. All my strength and power had vanished. It was just no good. I needed porn.

After thinking about the situation for a while, I decided the only thing to do was to go to a proper porn shop and buy a new set of mags. I'd hung around the one in the town centre a few times watching the men shuffle in and out with their heads pointing at the floor, but I'd always talked myself out of going in. Now I was there again, facing the same old fear but determined to do it. I needed porn, I needed it like oxygen.

The shop was dark and it took a couple of seconds for my eyes to adjust. Then it was Christmas. A big rush of colour and magic and pee-your pants excitement raced through me as I took in the rows of magazines, videos, and plastic dicks as big as babies' arms. Suddenly I was seven again, in my slippers and dressing gown, holding my daddy's hand and gasping with relief that Father Christmas had ignored my naughtiness and visited after all. I span round like a drunk, reaching out to touch a rubber cock to see if it was real.

'Is it a dildo you're looking for, mate?'

A freaky-looking bloke in a tracksuit, not much older than 21, appeared next to me, making me fart with fear. 'That's all we've got in at the moment but we can order from the catalogue.'

'I'm just looking for some mags,' I croaked out.

'Spank mags? They're on that shelf there. If it's spank mags you want I can do you a good deal. Fifteen quid each or three for twenty five.'

'What else is there?' I said, sounding as butch as Elmer Fudd.

He brushed against me, giving me the chance to sample his sweaty fragrance.

'This rack here,' he said, 'is a bit stronger.'

'What sort of stuff?'

'Well, that depends on what you're interested in. Big tits? Orgy? Big dick? Young girls? Cum shots?'

I nodded.

'Cum shots, eh? I can do you a really good deal. Three for forty. This one is very popular, a bit more expensive but if you bring it back in good condition I'll knock twenty off the next. Hardly ever see them come back, though. What about videos? I can do you some cracking vids. What type of vids do you like?'

'What can I get for a tenner, I've left me wallet at home and I've only got a tenner.'

His face changed. The Cheshire Cat grin disappeared and he put the mag he'd got me back on the shelf.

'Well, I'll tell you what, why don't you leave the tenner as a deposit, go home for your wallet and I'll do you a special deal?'

My guts had all but gone. I gave it one last try.

'I'll come back later, sure, but is there any mags I can get now for a tenner?'

The bloke thought for a moment.

'Only *Leather Fetish*. Don't you want nowt harder than that?'

I told him I'd take it.

He dropped underneath the counter and sprang back up again in two seconds flat with a load of photocopied papers stapled together. My heart sank. I handed over my tenner, my hand burning with the waste of it all, while he wrapped the papers up in brown paper and Sellotape.

'Cheers, mate.' he said. Then, as I was leaving. 'I'll see you again soon.'

I didn't dare open my package until I was alone, even though I was sure I'd been sold one big photocopied pup. I ran back to the house, not daring to peek at what I'd bought, and ripped it open the second I'd locked the door to my room. *The Leather Fetish* was just 22 pages of cheap black and white photocopy with printing that looked like it had been done on a newfangled typewriter circa the stone age. The cover had a fat granny with a rubber suit on it. Inside was pictures of granddaddies in leather and some old slappers, who must have all been sixty, with pierced nipples and thigh-high boots. I would have puked up me breakfast if I'd had any.

I read and re-read every last bit of writing and studied every picture trying to make the best of it, trying to squeeze an ounce of porn from the ten quid's worth of steaming hippo-shit the bloke had sold me. I had to use my imagination a lot, but after a while some of the contact ads started doing it for me enough to get it up. There were dozens of women just waiting for me to contact them and all I had to do was decide who would be the lucky one. A lot had this couples thing going, a lot wanted husbands to watch, and while both propositions seemed okay in the middle of a hand-shandy, they were dead scary in real life. The ones that got me really excited were the women on their own.

Most of them looked rough as fuck, even bearing in mind the photocopy quality and the thin black strip across their eyes.

All except one.

I didn't know about her at first but the more I looked, the more she came round. She was in her forties and was looking for a well-endowed young man for kinky games while hubby was away. I spent a couple of days wondering whether I should write to her, but all the time I knew she was going to get the nod. By the end of the week I was gagging for her small, stand-up tits and that dirty-ticket snarl that sent me into spasms of ecstasy whenever the Digger Barnes oil-well was ready to blow.

Finally I wrote her, Sue, a letter.

Hi, my name is Billy. I liked your ad and I think I'm just what you're looking for. I like it dirty as well so I think we are well suited. I've enclosed a picture of me on my holidays last year which I hope you like. Please write to me when your husband is going away and maybe we can have some fun. PS Please put it in a plain envelope and write 'private' on it.

I was amazed when I got her reply just two days later and when the time came I went there no problem. I had wanked over her letter until my balls ached. When you could still read it, the letter went.

Hi, Billy. You look gorgeous. Can't wait to see you in the flesh. Hubby will be away this Saturday. My address is (she put her address) just behind The Crown. If you drop around at about eight o'clock, the coast will be clear and we can have some fun. I'm sure you'll bring your own stuff but I've got some of my own. Why not bring your girlfriend as well? Can't wait to see you. xxx

She answered the door in a see-through negligée. Her face was harder than the picture and stuck in it was a fag puffed right down to the filter. She was old, maybe 50, but I could see her tits and there wasn't a second when I didn't think that this was the most exciting moment in history.

'You must be Billy,' she said, moving back to let me in. I could feel sweat forming on my back and forehead and my dick getting hard.

'Yes. Billy,' I answered and it must have come out all funny because she laughed.

'Well, are you coming in or not?' she asked taking another puff of the fag even though there was none of it left. I nodded and went through the small hallway, standing at the bottom of the stairs. Still chuckling she made her way through into the living room, wagging her finger at me to follow. She pointed to the sofa for me to sit down, but I stood by the edge looking at her.

'Well, Billy. You look just good enough to eat. Drink?'

I nodded again and she went over to the sideboard where there was a small selection of bottles on a silver tray.

'I always drink vodka and orange, would you like one?'

I said sure and she poured us both a drink as I soaked up the cheap red wallpaper, the dim lights and the picture of a naked woman on one wall and a tiger on the other.

'Not bring your girlfriend?' she asked handing me my drink.

I shook my head and took a swig. It tasted sharp and bitter and the alcohol made my head buzz.

'So, she doesn't know you've come here tonight? Does anyone else know? Tell your mates?'

I told her No which made her smile.

'Well,' she said, putting her drink down. 'What do you think? Not bad for an old girl, eh?'

She lifted back the straps of her negligée and let me have a good look at her tits. They were sagging a bit but the smallness of them kept them respectable and, you had to admit, she had good, long nipples.

'Why don't you bring your drink upstairs?' she said, laughing. 'I really hate small talk. I'm the kind of girl who just likes to get right down to it. Not like some people, all they want to do is talk. I'm not like that and I reckon you're probably the strong silent type.'

I said nothing as I followed her upstairs with my dick nearly bursting out of my pants. It was pitch black and I could only vaguely make out her shape as she moved through the bedroom to the huge double-bed.

'Take off your clothes and lie down. Are you sure no one knows you're here?'

'No one, honestly,' I said, stripping off my clothes as quickly as I could and lying on the bed. She slid towards me and took hold of my cock.

'Would you like to pretend I'm your mummy? Do you like fucking mummy? Mum's going to show you her little fairy.'

I wanted her to let my pistol go because I felt sure it was going to go off any minute. I think she sensed this because she moved her hand onto my chest.

'You're young enough to be my baby boy. I always wanted a baby but my husband can't have them. Have you got any brothers and sisters?'

'I'm an only child,' I said.

'Then you're all alone, just like me. Don't worry, mummy will take care of you. You remind me of a boy I used to know years ago. He had a cheeky smile, just like you.'

She sat next to my head and gently guided it to her crotch which smelt like soggy crab-paste sandwiches. I stuck my tongue out and started to lick, but got hair stuck in my mouth. I moved onto my knees and tried to stick my dick in her but she pushed me back and stuck my head back between her legs.

'Don't worry, sweetheart,' she said. 'There's plenty of time for whatever you want. You just stay where you are and swing your arse. That's it. Left to right, left to right.'

She began to grip tighter.

'Swing your little bum. Be a good boy for mummy and don't think about a thing.'

I heard something behind me and tried to pull up. She wrenched me back by the hair. A heavy arm wrapped around my waist and I felt something pushing against my arse. I struggled to get free but Sue still had hold of my head and the hairy arm was squeezing all the breath out of my stomach as a finger or thumb found its way up my hole. I shouted out but the arm choked my screams and forced my face deep into the mattress.

'Stay still or I'll beat the shit out of you. Stay fucking still.'

It was a man's voice. I froze as he replaced the thumb with something bigger which felt like a javelin. I screamed and screamed and cried and begged but he shoved it in faster and faster until I felt a hot burst of liquid inside followed by a shove to the floor.

'Don't move,' said the man, a troll-like geezer with thick curly hair. I wasn't going anywhere. I couldn't move. A load of feelings were running around my head and all crashing into each other, so much so that I couldn't think or feel anything other than empty.

'If he goes to the police...' said the man to Sue. 'You know we can't take any chances. If they start poking their noses in...'

Oh, Jesus. Sue nodded sadly. I had to do something clever and fast. I had to act happy.

'That was great,' I said, my teeth chattering beneath a shit-eating smile. 'I reckon I'll need the toilet for a minute, where is it?'

The man looked at me like I'd just arrived in a puff of smoke. I winked at him.

'I'm Billy. Nice to meet you.'

The fella looked at Sue who shrugged her shoulders and raised her eyebrows. He stood there not saying anything for a while so I spoke again.

'The toilet? Is it down the corridor?'

'On the right,' he said.

'Thanks big fella,' I said brushing past him. This seemed to annoy him a little because his eyes flashed but Sue took his arm and told him to go downstairs and make us all a drink.

I sat in the bathroom gasping for breath. Sue and the man were talking outside but I couldn't hear what they were saying. They were arguing, then they stopped. Finally Sue knocked on the door.

'You all right in there?'

I squeaked out a Yes, then concentrated before I opened my mouth again.

'I wouldn't mind a shower actually, got any towels?'

She opened the bathroom door ajar and stuck her arm through, pointing at a cupboard.

'In there,' she said. 'And there's some shower gel in the cupboard. Are you hungry? I can make a sandwich if you like.'

I said that would be great and she closed the door and went downstairs. I put the shower on but didn't get in it. I'd seen Psycho too many times to fall for that old trick. Instead I took off my clothes and rubbed myself down with a flannel, pouring a beaker of water over my head. My arse felt like it was bleeding and I stuck a load of tissue up it and had a bit of a cry. At first I thought I'd make a break for it through the bathroom window then decided against it. My best bet was to try and stick it out, get away without a chase. If he caught me trying to get down the drainpipe it'd be the end for sure. I had to stay cool.

I got dressed again and came downstairs. The man, whose name was Frank, her husband, was twisting the top off a bottle of Scotch. He nodded to a chair and I sat down as Sue handed me a cheese and ham sandwich and a shot of whisky.

'Hey,' I said. 'This is the five-star treatment. Some places they kick you out as soon as you've done it.'

Sue shook her head in disgust.

'I know, it's terrible the way some people carry on. Frank and I like to look on people as our guests, we're people persons me and Frank, aren't we, darling?'

'We like to make people welcome,' said Frank with a cold voice.

'How's your drink?' said Sue. 'I prefer a bit of plonk myself but Frank loves his Scotch.'

I said it was okay and the sandwich was first-class. Frank came and sat opposite me.

'Do you do this sort of thing a lot?'

'Yeah, now and again. I just like meeting new people. My kind of people.'

Sue murmured agreement. 'It's so hard to find broad-minded people these days. We're people persons me and Frank. We like people,'

'You look very young,' said Frank. 'How old are you?'

The drink was burning my tongue a bit. I had to think.

'Twenty. They call me baby face. I hope my struggling didn't put you off. I like to fantasise about being raped, did you mind?'

Frank grunted a laugh but said no more.

'You've got to be careful,' said Sue. 'There was a couple we met in Greece who said they were our sort then screamed blue murder when it came to the crunch. Didn't they, Frank?'

Frank just watched me.

I sat there and listened and listened to Sue and laughed in all the right places and even told a dirty joke. All the time I had my eye on the clock, reckoning about twenty to twenty-five minutes of conversation and another drink would put me in the clear. Eventually I said I'd have to leave.

'So soon,' said Sue. 'Don't you fancy staying the night?'

'No I better get back to the girlfriend. She doesn't know I do this sort of thing. It's not her sort of thing,' I said.

Sue laughed and told me to drop by with my girlfriend anytime.

'I'll have a little chat with her and talk her round. I'm very persuasive,' she said.

Frank walked me to the gate. As I went to leave, he put a hand on my shoulder.

'I don't want to see you here again. If I hear you've breathed a word about this to anyone, you'll know about it soon enough. My wife's a thicko but I'm not and I know a lot of people who could fuck up your life.'

He shook hands roughly.

'Remember, sonny. Not a word.'

It was a long walk home.

Bert and the Bees

(Extract from the novel 'God's Boxer')

It had been another nightmare night in the steak house. We'd cleared about two million meals and the rush-hour heat had nearly finished me off. The boss said we could have ten minutes off so me and the other chef, a bloke called Bert, splashed some water on our faces and went out in the yard for a smoke.

Bert made everyone laugh. He couldn't read to save his life, but if you gave that boy the right tools for the job he would fix just about anything for you. Okay, maybe I'm building him up a bit. I should have said that Bert could fix anything, but it was probably him that broke it in the first place. The boy was what you'd call a mystery of science. To most people he speaks no known language and I'm probably the only person who really understands him. Basically it was a short grunt for yes and a long grunt for no. A series of grunts followed by a laugh with wide-open eyes meant that he thought something was funny. An excited outburst followed by a wave of hands meant something was wrong, and a low couple of grunts with his chin buried in his chest means he's sad but doesn't want to talk about it. Bert looked like James Dean, but James Dean after being in fights all his life, eating nothing but chips, and living in an attic with no one to talk to.

That was the trouble with working full time in a place like this, your social life went out of the window and even when you did get a night off it didn't matter how much you washed your hair or scrubbed yourself, people could always smell that grease and meat. And what was the point of going out anyway? The only person I could call a friend was Bert and I couldn't say I knew that much about him. I said nothing as we sat in the yard. He said nothing either. We just sat on the empty beer barrels sipping pints of bitter shandy and looking at the last of the late summer light. We never really talked outside of the kitchen. I was 19-years-old and pretty damn lonely.

The boss shouted us back in and the three of us went to work. Soon the sweat was pouring off my forehead and Bert's shirt was sticking to him all over. The boss looked like some kind of volcano. His face was bright red and there was a big wet stain up his crack. Every five minutes or so he'd stick his head out the kitchen and call for a tray of bitter shandies. Then it went to lager with ice, then ice with lager. We drank and drank but the boss was still suffering. He got in a nark with Bert and clipped him round the ear then got me hacking up ribs only to switch me onto cutting garlic which was the job I hated most.

'Have you noticed,' I said to Bert. 'That the world's not as happy a place as it was when we were children? I never used to have a care in the world. Life was one long playtime. Now all I do is work and sleep and there's nothing in between, like some monster has sucked all the joy out of my life. Why is it?'

Bert shook his head.

'Not seen nothing like that but I've noticed something fucking weird,' he said.

I put down my knife and moved closer. Bert might be an idiot but maybe he had something earth-shattering to say. Sometimes you're so busy looking for answers that never come it takes someone like Bert to just blow you out of the sand.

'What have you noticed?' I asked.

'Bees,' he said. 'Bees and them fucking wasps and flies, but not so much when it comes to flies.'

As often is the case, Bert had me totally confused. My heart sank. He was talking crap.

'What about bees?' I asked. 'What the fuck have they got to do with anything?'

'Well, it's, like, summer and where are all the bees? The yard is always full of bees and that in the summer and flies. But there's only a few flies and there's no bees.'

'Maybe they've gone somewhere else,' I said.

'Nah,' said Bert. 'I've been looking out for them everywhere. On me days off I've been down to the park looking for bees and I'll tell you something, I haven't seen one fucking bee at all. Not one. And no wasps either.'

'Well I'm made up. I fucking hate bees.'

'Nah, bees is all right. Don't you know nothing? Bees make flowers and honey and that and if all the bees are gone then all the flowers will go as well and that means no more flowers and that means no more veggies. And cows eat flowers so there'll be no more cows and that'll mean sausages will go up in price 'cause that's all we'll eat. Fish. Is that all you want for your dinner every night forever? Do you want fish for breakfast? Do you think that's all right, like?'

'There must be bees about.'

'No, I'm not messing. It's been summer for weeks and no

bees. I've seen one dead one. One bee and that's it.'

'Imagine a world with no flowers,' I said.

'Who gives a shit about flowers? It's cows I'm worried about. If there's no cows then no money. No job. Are you a fucking nob or what? No bees, no money, and fucking fish all the way. Roast fish?'

Bert had worked himself up into a red-faced wreck. And as he began chopping up some lettuce, he had a real lump in his throat.

'I wouldn't mind,' he said, his eyes all wet. 'I don't care if there's no wasps. I fucking hate wasps, they sting you for no reason. But bees only sting if you're trying to get them. Bees is all right, nothing wrong with bees.'

The boss came in and pulled half-a-dozen steaks out of the fridge, dropping them on my counter.

'Hey, plums, back to work. There's a big table coming in now.'

'Boss, have you seen any bees about recently?' I asked.

'No. Fucking hate them.'

Bert slung down his knife and turned to argue but the boss made a fist and Bert went back to work. He never said another word all night, just mumbled to himself and slammed everything he got his hands on until I said 'I reckon bees are all right'. Then he was okay.

I walked home the same way as Bert even though it meant a longer journey because I hated going home on my own back to my crappy digs. My landlady was like some sort of creature from Hell while Bert lived in a council house all by himself which was such a sweet fucking deal that he wouldn't tell anyone how he landed it. About halfway between the restaurant and his house, Bert started getting all excited, saying something about coming in to have a go on his Commando Copter game and eat some toast. Actually, he asked if I wanted to eat Commando Copter and play on his toast but you get used to this sort of thing with him. It wasn't the first time he'd made such an invitation but usually I said no way. That's just the sort of twat I am. But tonight was different. I decided that Commando Copter, a game I'd played a lot in the arcade, had to be better than sitting alone in my digs, looking at the ceiling and listening to the bloke next door cough up his guts all night. So I smiled and said sure, which sent Bert into rapture. He legged it up to his front door, burst into the house and started jumping around on the sofa. He left to go and make the toast while I sat down and looked around the place. The room was blood red. He only had one lamp and that was in the shape of a football player heading a ball. The ball was all lit up and looked pretty good. But I knew from experience that you couldn't leave those lamps on for too long because the ball got really hot and made the whole room smell like fish. So I turned the lamp off and sat there in the dark waiting for Bert to come back.

I must have nodded off for a minute because I suddenly shook and saw Bert making 'Ka-pow' noises at a TV screen that was full of helicopters and explosions. He was doing well and I shouted encouragement. He turned round and gave me this really lovely smile but the lapse in concentration got him killed. He was pissed off and I sympathised with him because he'd got all the way to level 14 which was the IRA level. What you had to do is shoot all the terrorists and rescue the British hostages. The terrorists looked cool. They had black sunglasses and leather jackets and made these piercing death screams when they died. But the really fun thing to do was to ignore the terrorists and kill the hostages. When they died they barked out, 'Kill me, but spare my children.'

I turned my attention to a big plate of toast that was perched on the coffee table. It had gone cold and hard so I spat a big mouthful onto the carpet. Bert thought this was real hot shit and did the same. Pretty soon we were having a competition to see who could spit toast the furthest. We were getting really good at this when the toast ran out.

'You don't worry. I'll make some more and some tea,' he said.

He went into the kitchen and shouted something about not falling asleep again.

When he returned we both began spitting toast at the walls

and then at a beat-up tin bin with pictures of black horses on it. When we ran out of toast we used bits of old newspaper and that was fun for a while. Then we drank our tea.

'Want to know about my dad?' said Bert. 'He was like a boss dad and he lived here with me and me mum and me brother. Then one day I get home, sent home from school, like, and he's sitting down in the front room by himself and he's got me this remote control car and he says I'm an all right lad. He watches me take it out of the box and laughs as I leg out into the back yard with it. Then when I get back he's gone and then I never saw him again. He ran off with another woman everyone reckons.'

'What about your mum?' I asked.

'She's dead cause I burnt the house down,' he said.

'Burnt the house down? No messing? I mean, no fucking shit? Was you drunk or what?'

'Nah. I put some chips on after work, it was about two years ago I reckon, and fell asleep and when I woke up the house was all burning and the fireman brought me out in the garden and me brother was thumping me like mad.'

'And your mum died in the fire?'

'Nah. She got run over outside my auntie's house where we was living while the house got done up. My brother blamed me for the whole thing and now he won't even speak to me. He's working down south now but when he comes back I'll have to get out. I'll have nowhere to go then...'

His voice trailed off and I could see tiny tears forming in his eyes, he scrunched them up and looked away. I moved towards him and put a hand on his shoulder. He didn't move, my hand stayed there and I realised how broad and strong his shoulder was and my heart started beating faster and faster.

Bert started biting his nails, looking at nothing in particular.

'You could come and live in the boarding house with me,' I said.

Bert grunted.

'With that landlady you're always going on about? I've heard you say she's a loony. You say so yourself. You never stop going on about what a mad cow she is.'

'Okay, the landlady's a bit of a psycho. But if there were two of us there then we could look out for each other. The food's great – big breakfast and dinner – everything's free and it's dead cheap, only thirty a week. We could cover up for each other; keep a look-out when we wanted to sneak in and out. We'd be running rings around her.'

'I dunno.'

'She's not that bad once you get to know her, sometimes she's brilliant. She can do all these things like tell fortunes and that. She even taught me how to read tea leaves so that when you've finished your tea, you can look at the leaves and you can see things in them like me and you being really good friends and living in the same house and stuff.'

'How do you do it?'

'Well, when you've almost finished your tea, you leave a bit in the bottom and turn it over into a saucer and all these little shapes will appear that tell the future.'

Bert went and got a saucer from the kitchen tipped the dregs of tea into it and stuck his nose in. I said it wouldn't work if he used tea bags but he said his family had always stuck with leaves.

'I can't see a fucking thing. Look it's, like, just a load of tea on a plate. There's nothing on this plate but old tea mashed up. Tea's for drinking. You can't tell nothing from tea.

I took the saucer.

'You're wrong Bert. You're in the tea. And its saying that if you move to my place it'll be the luckiest thing you ever do, you'll get loads of money, like winning the lottery or something. It's amazing. I can see it all.'

'Fucking yes. Them tea leaves are fucking magic,' said Bert. 'Do you reckon it will really happen?'

'The tea never lies.'

'Fucking hell. It'll be brilliant. I'll buy me own house and you can come and stay there and I'll get some of them bee hives so we can have honey every day and I'll get us two lawn-mowers the kind you can sit on and we'll race them all around the house. It'll have a massive garden and I'll make sure the grass never gets cut so we can race around on our lawn-mowers all day. I'll get a red one and you'll have a blue one and I'll even get us a Cup – like the FA Cup but for lawn-mower racing and we could even get other people to come and race against our team. It'll be fucking amazing. I've heard them sit-on mowers go 35. That's more than a normal car in the street.'

'That's right, Bert. All you've got to do is come with me.'

'What does your tea say?' he asked, his eyes glowing.

I lifted up my cup and saw what looked like a bee.

Frank Dullaghan

Crossing

It was some years ago.
The fields had tucked
themselves in for the night
and the sky could hardly
keep its eye open.

There were no markers,
the grey of one holding
spilled into the next.
The high hedges pushed
the road over the hills.

Light cracked a corner.
On the straight
a man waved a lamp, a gun
black in his other hand.
The road stopped

to slow shadows,
balaclavas, eyes,
unblinking muzzles.
At the lowered window
a mouth smoked words,

ordinary words
familiar to an ear
at any border crossing –
Where are you travelling?
Where have you come from?

But here, out of nowhere;
out of the flat slap

of trees against windscreen;
the settled hum of the mind:
terror.

Not that anything had happened –
the licence taken,
noted as British;
my accent – *Border boy,*
home on holidays, are you?

It was the way the quiet
wrapped about us;
his clean blue eyes;
the slowness of his hand
returning my papers.

Ordnance Survey 24 – West Cork

Hungry Hill, Derryclancy, Coombane –
high names in her silent room,
his dinner cold on the table,
the clock slowly wiping its face –
Claddaghgarriff, Knockowen, Rams Hill.

The quiet life. The long tick of the room.
And now this unfolding
of an old map, the wood grain
stain of a mountain range,
her finger touching each town.

The moon is loud on the road;
her right hand cold on the pane,
frozen like five points of a star
when she reached out to his falling.
Now he sways at the gate, singing.

In her other hand the mountains
are folded away – West Cork –
the breadth of the Irish sea
between the one hand and the other.
The names are packed in her head:
Rams Hill, Knockowen, Claddaghgarriff,
Coombane, Derryclancy, Hungry Hill.

Escalator

Hold me she asked
turning on the escalator,
against the cold
and he wrapped his arms about her
hesitantly,
embarrassed someone might see
his arms around this woman
descending the escalator
into the city.
But his arms
took on a will of their own
as her head nestled like a bird
under his breast bone
and her hair-tips teased
his interlocked fingers.
He held her tenderly,
a boy with a fledgling,
his heart counting the seconds
till the escalator would slip
like a knife
under the footpath,
his arms fall away
and his eyes watch her
walk off into the city.

Frames

(i) We are in our small square kitchen
  laughing with daddy
  who sits enthroned in his corner
  beneath the blue and gold of Our Lady;
  the shelf with his rack of Peterson pipes,
  his books – *Electrical Engineering,*
  The Imitation of Christ.
  The radio crackles a jig
  and the shine on his boot winks
  as he reaches out for mammy,
  pulls her onto his knee.
  We are all caught in this extravagance –
  my plump mother bounced,
  her face flushed, pushing herself up, 'Tommy!'
  her mouth cross, her eyes dancing.

(ii) I leap the banisters,
  landing crouched as a wrestler in the door-frame.
  Daddy, red-faced, stands with belt fisted,
  my young brother in the vice of his other hand.
  His anger is a great moment of silence.
  I notice the tremor in his shoulders;
  the power in his face.
  My skinny frame challenges his bulk.
  My head is somewhere else
  watching myself circle and shout,
  my own hands balled, my chest tight.
  'So you're old enough now?' he retorts,
  blocking the door as I take my brother's hand.
  Yet he steps back from the fight and I pass
  thinking somehow that I've won.

(iii) Daddy came home to his mother
  in the brown of a Franciscan friar's habit
  to kneel in bare-sandelled feet

by his father's death bed.
Eldest of six, he stayed on
as provider, apprentice electrician,
in steel-toed boots. Hating it.
Years later he showed me
the soft white length of rope he'd kept
coiled on the back shelf of his wardrobe
like a snake tempting his return
to a cloister's silence
from the duty he'd bound himself to.
He held it up between us
in his wide-opened palms.

Richard John Evans
Time

I suppose I've always been interested in time travel, really. The funny thing is, in *Star Trek* – the original series, I mean – there are very few storylines that actually deal with time travel. Surprisingly few, given that the series was constantly exploring all the science fiction basics that had been around for years in novels and short stories. The only really memorable one is when the Enterprise goes through a wormhole and appears in the Earth sky in the twentieth century and is picked up by America and Russia's radars as a potential nuclear attack. Proper Cold War stuff, you know. Then there's the film, obviously, the fourth one, when they take the Klingon ship back in time and visit present day America. But it's a really shit film, that one, confirming the old theory that *Star Trek* films alternate fairly precisely between really good and really bad. I've got them all on video, and if you watch them all in one go you can see exactly what I mean: the first one is, at the end of the day, pretty crap. The sequel, with Ricardo Montalban as the vengeful Khan and Spock dying at the end was brilliant. Then you've got a *Star Trek III, The Search for Spock*, which is really disappointing. Actually, that screws up the theory, because the fourth one – *The Journey Home* – is rubbish too.

But anyway, yeah, time travel. I'm always thinking about it. Like now, right, I'm looking across the room, sort of taking it all in, and I'm kind of aware of a sense of motion. But not real motion, like a physical movement, but of movement through time. My flat is travelling forward in time, at a rate of one second per second. It's true, it's undeniable but most people would look at you funny if you put it that way. But I can almost feel it. And now, as the flat ploughs slowly onward, aiming for morning, it feels like I just need to reach out a little bit with my mind and I can change things. The rate of forward momentum. The direction of movement. I like that feeling. It's like being in a little module of my own.

When we eventually arrive at morning, my giro will come through the letterbox. I'll go to the post office to cash it, get some electric, get some gas, pay my sister what I owe her then go down to Cardiff. Forbidden Planet's good. It just opened about a year ago. It's mainly a comic shop but it's got the best science fiction book selection I've ever seen. I usually go there first. They've got a lot of *Star Trek*-related stuff there and a lot of it's very good – novelisations, comics, fanzines and that. I can find out what's the latest on all this talk about a new *Star Trek* series. It's been in the pipeline for ages. It's meant to be like the next generation of Star Fleet people in an up-dated version of the Enterprise. I'll probably spend a fortune in Forbidden Planet. I usually end up spending most of my giro and having nothing left for food and stuff. I tend to borrow off my sister Sarah for the rest of the fortnight. Mind you, she won't have much to spare this week – Karl's staying over because Amanda, my other sister, is in hospital.

Time travel, then, and this novel I'm writing. It's about this machine that can travel backwards in time but only once every twenty years. So what it does is accumulates all the technological advances of those twenty years then, when the time comes, goes back and incorporates all this stuff into its original design. So by the time it's actually switched on for the first time, it's far more advanced and powerful than the people who invented it could have imagined. The novel's influenced by some of Asimov's robot stories, you know, computer logic and all that. But it's also going to be a bit like Robert Heinlein's stuff because it's got quite a clever time paradox in it and he's good at them. Basically, if the machine's grabbing all this hi-tech gear and welding it on to the original version of itself, then it doesn't need to go looking for the stuff when it's switched on – it's already there. I mean, there's more to the story than that. I haven't worked out an ending for it yet and I've got to get some characters to put in it. But the basics are there.

I'm writing it out at the moment but I'm going to type it

up eventually. My sister's boyfriend, Johnny, gave me an electric typewriter a few months ago. He didn't want any money for it either. Just as well really. Then my other sister, Sarah, pointed at the fluorescent writing on the back of it. Turned out it's property of my old school. I had to laugh. That's Johnny for you. That's what he does. When he and Amanda got their own council flat he nicked a telly and video for them. Then Amanda had Karl so he stole a pram from outside Spar. Amanda said thank Christ he checked there wasn't a baby in it and Johnny said he hadn't. Just lucky, he said. We all had to laugh at that. He used to be all right, though, Johnny. You wouldn't trust him, like, but he was a good laugh and took everything pretty easy. But back then he only used to do draw and whizz or a few Es. Now he's on smack – even though he keeps saying he's packed it in – and that's where all his money from nicking stuff goes. And he's just not interested in having a laugh or anything anymore. He can get pretty nasty, these days, Johnny.

Just been watching a bit of telly. This special news bulletin came on all about Thatcher resigning. So I put *The Empire Strikes Back* on the video and I had a thought. Basically, even though the *Star Wars* trilogy is more visually compelling and complete, *Star Trek* will always be the more intellectually rewarding. Because the *Star Wars* stuff is based on a childishly simple premise – good against evil. Now in *Star Trek* – well, fair enough, you've got the Klingons. But look at it logically – they're a race of beings who happen to be aggressive and expansionist and warlike. What's far-fetched about that? We've got plenty of them on Earth right now. Quite a few episodes are about potential peace talks and treaties between Star Fleet and the Klingons, usually with the Romulans involved too. It's just like the Cold War, or Palestine and Israel, or even Northern Ireland. There's no discussion of the political philosophy behind The Empire in *Star Wars*. They just go around being really heavy and blowing up whole planets. But I'll be the first to admit that Lucas did an absolutely amazing job at creating the *feel* of an alien galaxy. You do actually feel you're looking at a real place. All the spaceships look battered and grimy. Everything's squeaky clean on board *Star Trek* ships. And look at the *Star Wars* robots – totally utilitarian and convincing.

I'm always hungry this time of night so I'm going to make some food in a minute. We've got some potatoes, some beans and some bread. So I'll have a bit of boiled potatoes and toasted bean sandwiches. I can hear Joni crying in the next room now. She's Sarah's baby. She's about a year old, or perhaps a bit more, or perhaps not quite that much. Sarah's boyfriend, Lee, drives a JCB. They've put in for a flat like Amanda and Johnny and they're on the list. It's a pretty full house here at the moment – me, Sarah, Lee, Joni and Karl, who's here because Amanda's in hospital and nobody knows where Johnny is. Sarah phoned his mother and Lee went round the pubs but nobody's seen him.

Just remembered – there should be another cheque in the post for me in the morning as well as my giro. There's a science fiction fanzine called *Tralfamadore* and I do some reviews for them from time to time. I did one not long ago. It's funny, really, because the book they sent me to review was by William Gibson, who does all that Cyberpunk stuff and I'm not that keen usually. But this one was really good. It had a bit of time travel in it, sort of. But it's all virtual reality, so it's not necessarily the actual, objective truth. That's my main beef with the whole Cyberpunk thing, really. All very well to explore the virtual world inside the computer but if the character, say, goes back in time and it goes on for pages and you're really getting into it, it's really disappointing when it turns out it was all virtual anyway so it didn't really, actually happen. I mean, what's the point? It's like those stories you used to write at school where everything was really far-fetched and, because you couldn't then pull out of it, you had to say 'and then I woke up – it had all been a dream' at the end. Still, I think my review was pretty fair and I should be getting the money for it tomorrow. A tenner I think. It all helps.

Tralfamadore's got quite a good circulation. You always see the new issue in Cardiff Library. It really pisses me off when people say there's only a small market for science fiction, like it's not a real type of writing or something. I used to go to this creative writing workshop every second Thursday in the community centre. The woman who ran it, Dee-Dee, really hated SF and fantasy. I mean, she didn't even like horror and every pleb likes horror, even if it's just Stephen King. So the whole thing was a bit of a waste of time for me. I mean, if the person looking at your stuff, this supposed expert, doesn't accept the genre you're working in, how can they be objective about it? Well, Dee-Dee said she wasn't inherently prejudiced against any kind of writing – except the stuff done by this funny old bloke called Pearce, which was fair play really – and she'd take each piece on its merit. But it's funny how she could never find anything good to say about my stuff. Someone else would write something really dreary about some married couple getting divorced or something and she'd love it, even if nothing happened in it, even if there were no ideas in it or anything. I just do my own thing now. I think I get on better that way, especially now I'm linked up with other people with similar interests.

Tick tick, one *s* per *s*. I've just put the potatoes on. I was standing there, peeling them, and I could really, seriously feel the time ticking through the kitchen. And, better still, through me. Then Sarah came in wearing her slippers, saying she'd just phoned the hospital. Amanda's sleeping. They say she'll be in for about a week. Still no sign of Johnny though. Sarah and Lee are going to take Karl up to the hospital tomorrow. Sarah's phoned our mother, up in Aberystwyth, but she can't come down. Gaz, her boyfriend, is working and she can't afford the bus fare. She moved up there about two or three years ago with Gaz and my two brothers. They were going to travel right through Britain in the camper, but it broke down in Aberystwyth so they just stayed there. When they went, the council started moving the rest of us out of the house and into flats, which was good, because now we've got central heating. And when Sarah and Lee get a place, I'll have the flat to myself.

When I've finished my novel the first person to see it will be Gary. He's one of my correspondents. He lives just outside

Bolton. I answered an ad he put in *Tralfamadore* some time last year or the year before asking if anyone had the last series of *Blake's 7* on video. As it happened, I did. I'm not a massive fan but some of the ideas were quite good, like this one about a planet covered in intelligent sand. So we've just kept writing to each other ever since. His letters are always about nine pages long, they're great. We test each other on *Star Trek* and stuff, and introduce each other to different writers. He's tried to get me into J.G. Ballard but I'm not that keen. It's not really SF as far as I can see. The ideas are really far-fetched and he never really explains them – you just get pages of people wandering around, lost, talking gibberish like they're on drugs. It's really pretentious. But the good thing about Gary is he's the only person I know who's read more than me, so he'll read my book and tell me if it's too much like something else. He's good at that.

Finished the food now, so I'm just lying on the mattress, letting it go down. I'm thinking about everybody else, above and below me here in Glanafon Flats, mostly asleep, all travelling with me through time. All in separate modules but all travelling at the same rate. I've got this image of my flat suddenly peeling off, accelerating away from them, or swerving into a u-turn and heading back or maybe even changing lanes altogether. That would be such a cool image, except how do you render it visually unless you translate the temporal into the spatial, like a metaphor? You can't do it, really, which is why I suppose not many film makers do time travel with any real imagination. Just whirling colours and all that crap.

I've got a little bag of Chewy Cola Bottles for later. I bought them with the last of my money. Well, there wasn't much else I could have done with it, a handful of fives. Just waiting to arrive at Giro-through-letterbox time now. I've got another Re-start interview when I sign on next Thursday. They ask you what you've been doing to find work. I'll be able to tell them about my book review. That should impress them. Shows I've been making the effort. Not just a job, the *right* job, as all their leaflets say. Actually, I've just had a thought.

Perhaps I'd better not tell them. Because I got paid for it. It's only a tenner but that might affect my dole. I'll just tell them I did it for free. I don't want any trouble – we've still got that Poll Tax thing hanging over our heads. You'd think they'd write it off by now. It was all a misunderstanding anyway. Neither of us have got a job, we're both on Income Support so we don't have to pay. I don't really know where we stand with the Council Tax though. I think we pay a percentage. Oh, and we've got the water rates as well, or some of them anyway. And I suppose we'd better think about the telly licence as well. But not tomorrow, no. It's Cardiff that money's destined for and the till at Forbidden Planet.

Lee was telling me about this supermarket they've just opened around here somewhere where you can get a tin of beans for something like ten pence. They're twenty eight in Happy Shopper. But there's thirteen and a half per cent extra at the moment so it goes further. I can't believe I'm seriously talking about beans. But there you go. That's my life – science fiction and beans. Nah, you've got to laugh. I'm not bothered. People can say what they like. It's better than working at some job I can't stand, coming home and watching shit on the telly because my mind's too fucked to realise how crap it is. This way I get to work on my book.

Joni's just started crying again and woken Karl up, so now they're both screaming their heads off. I call them the horrible homunculi for a laugh. Seriously though, how am I supposed to concentrate with all that going on? I've got this little like fantasy I go into sometimes, where I'm the only real human being on Earth, and all the other people are just androids, there to test my reactions. Then the people who designed the whole thing take notes and everything. The big test is whether I can finish this novel, in spite of everything they throw at me. It's amazing how cunning they have to be to maintain the illusion of reality, to make me think it's all real. Take this week for example. They've realised I can still read and write and do my work, even with Joni crying and Sarah and Lee watching some crap Tom Cruise film too loud in the other room. So they decide to put Karl here as well, to see if I can cope with that. Of course, they need a bit of back-story, they can't just dump him here randomly. So they arrange it so Amanda takes an overdose of contraceptive pills because Johnny got her pregnant again and she's in a bit of a state. And although that's an illogical act on Amanda's part, it appears totally realistic and natural to me, because they've led me to expect so-called human beings to do illogical things sometimes. It's an interesting fantasy and I like playing with it in my mind from time to time. Of course, it's already been done by quite a few writers, but I reckon I could probably do it better. Perhaps I'll do it for my second novel.

The crying has stopped and it's all quiet now. My telly's on with the sound down and my eyes are starting to feel all gritty and tired. So I'll switch the light off and just have a bit of a lie down on the mattress for a while. It'll be getting light soon.

Euron Griffith

themepark

It was an invasion. Huge trucks and digging machines rumbled like tanks through the villages and men in hard hats filled up the local caffs. Fights broke out in *The Flying Fox* and protest groups lined the entrance of the themepark site to try and stop the lorries. My mum said it reminded her of the miner's strike.

Wales Today arrived. They filmed a pitched battle between the police and the hippies which later won some kind of award. There were fifty arrests and one policeman lost an eye. The place was in chaos. And then the phone rang.

'It's Ed.'

I should have known.

'See it?'

'What?'

'The news.'

'Oh yeah. Terrible isn't it?'

I heard him pull hard on a cigarette.

'Ed,' I said, 'maybe we should back off.'

'No way!'

'But all these reports!'

'Meet me.'

'Where?'

'The pub.'

'When?'

'Now.'

The phone clunked and purred. I replaced the receiver and ran a comb through my hair. I looked a mess but the dole did that to you. I only shaved on Giro day. That was the only time I could afford to go out.

★

Ed was halfway through a Guinness when I arrived. He'd

bought me a Grolsch. I popped it open.

'It's sorted.'

'What, just like that?'

He smiled.

'Five weeks.'

'A bit quick.'

'It's business.'

Ed and me had history. We'd gone to school together, we'd smoked dope together, we'd picked up girls together, and we'd signed on together. In all that time I'd never heard him say a sentence that contained more than two words. Not that he was thick or anything. Far from it. He knew about the arts.

'What's the *Ancient Mariner* about?.

'A bird.'

'*Under Milk Wood*?'

'A village.'

'*Battleship Potemkin*?'

'A pram.'

He was a punk conversationalist.

He was also shrewd. As a kid he'd once stored snowballs in his mum's freezer during the winter and then sold them for twenty pence each in July.

'So what did they say?'

Ed shrugged.

'It's coming.'

'When?'

'August.'

'And they want us to do it?'

He nodded.

'Even though we've got no experience?'

He shrugged again. He reached into his pocket and took out a wad of papers which had been stapled together. He flattened it out on the table and handed me a pen.

'Sign.'

'What is it?'

'A contract.'

'With who?'

'With them.'

'What does it say?'
'Just sign.'
'Can't I read it first?'
'What for?'
'In case they rip us off!'
'They won't.'
'How do you know?'
He smiled.
'Trust me.'

It had all started with the camera. An uncle of mine had won a small fortune on the lottery and he came back to Wales to buy presents for his relatives. It was only the second time I'd met him and I felt a bit guilty as we stood in Dixons waiting for my mum to decide how many tellies she wanted.

'And what would *you* like Dean?' He spread out his arms as if he was showing me Arizona. 'Anything at all. My treat. Don't be shy.'

He had an awful fixed smile and I suddenly realized that this guy was feeling more guilty than me.

Guilty for having never written to my mother.

Guilty for having never returned for his father's funeral.

Guilty because he was rich.

And guilty because he'd just remembered my name wasn't Dean.

'I'll have *that.*'

I'd pointed at over five grand's worth of video equipment.

'Wrap it up,' said my uncle.

'Right away sir,' said the salesman.

Six weeks passed. The video equipment stayed in its boxes. They were piled up in the corner of my bedroom and covered with a sheet. One day, skint and in between Giros, I invited Ed round to see how much he reckoned I could get for it all in Muddy Taylor's Second Hand Shop. Ed sat on the edge of the bed and snapped a can of Heineken. I unveiled the boxes like a cheap magician and, when I turned around, Ed's face was white. His mouth had dropped open and Heineken froth was dripping down his arm.

'Ed, are you okay?'

He looked at me as if I'd just shown him a headless corpse. Then he gave a stunned little nod. He came over for a closer look.

'I could put it in the *Leader*,' I said, 'but I haven't got the readies. Do you think Muddy'd give me five hundred?'

'Five hundred?'

'Well, four then.'

'You're mad!'

'Well how much then? You tell me.'

'For this?'

'Yeah.'

'All in?'

'Yeah.'

'Jesus Christ!'

He turned away and faced the window. He took a sip of Heineken and I noticed that his hands were shaking.

'Ed, I –'

'Shut up.'

'What?'

'I'm thinking.'

I left him to it. That was the best way with Ed. Whatever he had to say he'd get round to it in the end. I went downstairs to make a pot of tea. The kettle was just about to boil when Ed thundered down the stairs. He entered the kitchen with an excited look on his face.

'Pink Rat,' he said.

Pink Rat used to be the school band but now they signed on like everyone else. Ed's plan was to do a promo for them and get it on to MTV. He'd always been obsessed with television and now, with my gear, I think he'd discovered his ticket out of the valleys.

We hired the hall of the old Miners' Institute for an afternoon and devoted three hours of tape to Pink Rat performing a song called 'Nuke the Vatican'. When we finished I needed a drink. Pink Rat said they'd buy us one.

The Flying Fox was full. Workmen from the themepark site

crowded the lounge and there was a row of hard hats and mobiles all along the bar. We went into the snug and sat next to a couple of hippies who were feeding crisps to a dog. When *Wales Today* came on we all looked up at the telly. Once again the scenes at the themepark site dominated everything. The reports showed workmen being driven into the park in buses. They were pelted with stones from the demonstrators and, when the cops moved in, there was a big fight. The reporter was jostled and the pictures got jerky. Someone held a hand up towards the lens and then there was a sharp edit. They returned to the studio and we returned to our beers.

'I went to a themepark once.' This was Del, the bass player. 'In Germany it was. They had a bunjee jump. Me and my sister did it. You jumped off this crane like. It was brilliant. I've got it on tape.'

A funny look came over Ed's face. His earlier despondency at the realization that Pink Rat were never going to make it onto MTV was suddenly swept away.

'On tape?'

'Yeah. VHS. They record your jump and sell it to you afterwards.'

'They're getting one here,' said the singer, 'I saw it in the *Leader*. BUNJEE JUMP SET FOR THEMEPARK. Some guys from Canada or something. It said they were millionaires.'

'This tape,' said Ed.

Del's face lit up.

'Would you like to see it?'

'Yes.'

'Okay, when?'

'Right now.'

From the moment he saw the rather blurry record of Del's bunjee jump, Ed was a man with a mission. He persuaded me to set up a meeting with Kevin Spray, the Amenities Manager at the themepark site. Ed reckoned that, with our video equipment, we could approach the owners of the Canadian bunjee jump with a business proposal. They provide the jump, we tape it. It didn't sound very convincing to me but the Amenities Manager seemed to like it. He said he'd follow it up and then he shook our hands. Once outside, Ed punched the air and shouted 'yes!' It was the first thing he'd said all afternoon. Now, a month later, here I was fiddling with the top of a Grolsch bottle in the snug of *The Flying Fox*.

'Just sign,' said Ed.

'Hang on.'

The stapled pad of contracts and waiver forms had been faxed to Kevin Spray's office that afternoon. A courier had then delivered them to Ed's mum's house and Ed, eager to get going, had signed them immediately. I flicked through some of the pages. The *Buffalo Dive Bunjee Crew* from Ontario could obviously afford good lawyers. Some of the small print was the size of bacteria.

'What's wrong?'

'Nothing. I'm just reading it through.'

Ed sighed wearily and drummed his fingers on the table. Then he stood up and went to the bar. I was relieved. It was impossible to think straight with him staring at me all the time.

'Want one?'

'No thanks, I'm fine.'

I held up the half-full Grolsch as evidence and returned to the stapled pad. I still couldn't concentrate though. The events of the past month kept racing through my head like newsreel. I thought about the big gang of ex-miners who had joined the Protest Group outside the themepark site gates. They were angry because they'd heard about a proposed new ride called 'The Big Shaft'. This was a Virtual Reality trip through the catacombs of a coalmine at high speed. A company from Japan had been busy for weeks putting the final touches to it. The ex-miners had pointed out that *The Miners' Heritage Centre,* which was only five miles away (and on which many of the men relied upon for their livelihoods), already *had* a virtual reality coalmine ride. They admitted that it wasn't exactly 'state of the art' but it was their most popular attraction and it brought in the crowds. 'The Big Shaft' represented unfair competition and the Centre might face closure. 'Nonsense,' said a man from the Tourist Board on

Wales Today, 'there is no reason why the Heritage Centre and the new themepark should not co-exist.' Later on in the same programme they dropped an item and returned 'live' to the themepark gates. Yushami Wakamoto, the Director of *Anatagata Virtual Reality (Japan) Ltd.*, had turned up unexpectedly and the place had erupted into violence. Ex-miners had broken through the security barriers and police with riot shields had been rushed in from Cardiff but they were too late to save Mr Wakamoto. He'd been taken to Merthyr General with suspected skull fracture. Apparently, an ex-miner had whacked him over the head with a lump of coal.

That's when ITN got interested.

A crew was sent down from London and they checked into the Guest House owned by Ed's mum. Dazzled by their gear and their sexy lifestyles, Ed hadn't been slow to make friends (although the Londoners were still slightly bemused by his unorthodox approach to conversation). He helped them load their gear every morning and, in return, Nick Hodges, the cameraman, had promised to show Ed a few tricks of the trade after they'd finished covering the protests. From that moment, Bruce Willis had been deposed as Ed's all-time hero and his vocabulary had been enriched by a new word. Nick.

'There's Nick!'

I looked up from the stapled pad. Nick Hodges and his soundguy had just walked in. Ed wiped a blob of Guinness foam from his upper lip, 'Hey, Nick!' Nick raised his arm in acknowledgement and he came over to join us. The soundguy followed with two lagers.

'Where's Julian?' asked Ed. Julian was the reporter.

'Talking to his missus on the mobile,' said the soundguy.

Nick raised his pint to his lips and adopted a conspiratorial tone.

'Problems at home.'

'Always happens,' said the soundguy, 'if he's away for more than two days Nicole's on the blower furious as fuck. You'd think she's understand by now.'

'Remember Sarajevo?'

'Shit,' said the soundguy, 'how could I forget!'

'That was the worst.'

'By far. It was tragic.'

'What happened?' asked Ed. He was like an eager puppy.

Nick and the soundguy looked at each other. They were wondering whether to tell the story or not. In the end the soundguy gave a what-the-hell shrug.

'We saw this old bloke,' he said, 'must have been at least seventy but he was dashing about like a teenager.'

'He was carrying a bucket,' said Nick, 'heading for the water-pump.'

The soundguy shook his head solemnly.

'Nobody does that.'

'Not in daylight.'

'Not in Sarajevo.'

'Anyway,' said Nick, 'I switched to record and we followed him. Julian came too. We reached the square and the old bloke stopped. The pump was on the other side. To reach it he'd have to run across thirty yards of exposed ground.'

'We knew he'd never make it,' said the soundguy.

'Those snipers were shit hot,' said Nick, 'they could clip the balls off a bluebottle.'

The soundguy leant forward.

'I had all the levels ready,' he said, 'gunshots can really fuck them up if you're not careful.'

Nick took over.

'The old bloke takes a deep breath and goes for it. He's halfway across, still swinging this stupid bucket, when –'

He looked away in sadness and disgust. He picked up his lager and sipped it slowly. Ed was on tenterhooks. He turned to the soundguy.

'When what?'

The soundguy looked at Nick and sighed heavily.

'Julian's fucking mobile went.'

'I had him as well,' said Nick, desperately trying to contain his anger, 'right in the middle of frame. The bullet gets grandad in the hip and he goes sprawling. It was a beautiful shot. I even had the upturned bucket in focus but, just as the slug is fired, what do I hear, loud as a fucking bell? *Nicole, not now sweetheart, I'm busy.* I mean, Jesus Christ!!'

'Shouldn't call him at work,' said the soundguy.

'That would have been a BAFTA winner,' said Nick, 'no doubt about it. Instead, some bastard from the Beeb got it for some shit about Rwanda. Anyone could do that. Starving kids are easy. All you've got to do is lock off the camera and fill the fucking frame!'

'Julian was very apologetic,' said the soundguy, 'but it was too late. The old guy was bleeding like a pig and screaming his head off. ITN would never have cleared it. Too upsetting. We carried on recording for a bit. We reckoned that if the sniper tried to finish the job we might be able to dub the second shot over the first one but no such joy. An ambulance arrived and it fucked up all the levels.'

He looked at Nick rather nervously.

'Fancy a scotch?'

Nick gave a serious little nod and the soundguy stood up. 'Would you lads like anything?'

I told him we were fine and he went off to the bar with a twenty pound note. Ed took the stapled pad from me with a smile. Stunned by the story, I'd signed it without thinking.

Three months passed. Mr Wakamoto recovered and went back to Japan wearing a turban. The protests dwindled and ITN lost interest. Nick and the crew were recalled to London.

In late April the themepark opened to the public and became an instant success. Queues formed at eight o'clock in the morning and, after a few weeks, permission was granted by the council to build an overflow coach parking area. Tony Blair came and bought a candy floss. Two days later William Hague won an enormous panda on the Virtual Reality Coconut Shy. The village was crowded again. Ed's mum drew up plans for an extension to the Guest House and Betty from *The Flying Fox* bought a Mercedes convertible on the proceeds of her steak and kidney pudding.

Me and Ed were doing well too.

In our first month we made enough money to rent a large flat above the Rediffusion showroom. I signed off, got myself a credit card, opened a saver's account to prepare for the quiet winter months, and I splashed out on an Armani suit from a posh shop in Cardiff. At first I'd been worried about signing a contract with the Canadians but, in practice, everything was cool.

The bunjee ride cost fifty quid.

The video was twenty five.

Twenty of that was ours.

With anything up to forty punters a day Ed and me were making a fortune.

But Ed wasn't happy.

Filming hysterical Germans and Americans as they hurtled to an abrupt bounce just twenty feet away from certain death wasn't good enough for him. The ITN crew had impressed him and he was now more desperate than ever to become a professional news cameraman. He applied for a trainee place with BBC Wales but he didn't even get an interview. I tried to tell him that you needed a degree to get into television but Ed wouldn't listen. He'd got the bug. He wanted to go to Bosnia with Kate Adie. He wanted to huddle in the back of a Land Rover filming one of John Simpson's pieces to camera.

One day I turned up at our video podium at the park to find Ed and the camera missing. There was a note on the table in our makeshift office. It said 'back soon'.

I had to fob off the punters all day with a lie about 'technical difficulties' but I don't think I was very convincing.

Ed turned up later in *The Flying Fox*. Apparently there had been a fire at a tyre warehouse in Barry and he'd gone there with the camera hoping to film it for *Wales Today* before their regular crew arrived. 'Amateur footage,' he said.

None of it got used.

The Canadians were furious when they heard about it. One more stunt like that, they said, and they'd sue us for breach of contract.

'Fuck them,' said Ed.

We went back to the flat and watched 'Mad Max' on our new Sony widescreen.

★

Ten days after the public opening there was an 'official' opening and all the themepark amenities staff received letters from Kevin Spray telling us to dress smartly because Prince Charles was turning up. I wore my Armani suit and stood next to Ed at the end of a long line as we waited our turn to shake hands with the Royal Party. The Party consisted of Prince Charles, Prince William, and Sheik Zair Al-Haddid.

The Sheik was sixteen and was Prince William's best friend at Eton. All through the late winter and early spring the tabloids had printed feature after feature about the new Royal Chum. There had been photos of his palace in Kuwait, his flat in Kensington, his silver-plated Bentley, and the birthday cake in the shape of an oil-rig that he'd received from his father, Harif Al-Haddid, the twelfth richest man in the world. *The Sun* had even printed 'Ten Things you Never Knew About Our Willie's Little Pal'. The list included, at number six:

> *Zair Al-Haddid's full name is Zair Beyerty Hannad Mustaf Best Charlton Law Muhammad Al-Haddid. His dad is a big Man Utd fan.*

The two friends were now following Prince Charles as Kevin Spray led him along the parade of amenities staff. At every fourth person or so the Prince would stop and have a brief chat. The routine was a well-practised one.

He'd laugh.

He'd look serious and ask a question.

He'd nod.

He'd crack the illusion of a private joke and then he'd walk off, tugging at his cuff-links and half-turning to give the impression that he'd love a longer chat but time was against him.

Behind the ticker-tape line about twenty yards away the photographers clicked and whirred like a jungle. Some of them were standing on step-ladders and begging Prince William or the Sheik to give them a smile.

Ed was furious. All morning he'd been hearing reports of a

massive pile-up on the Severn Bridge. He wanted to sneak off and film the casualties with our new digi-cam but it was impossible to move. There were security guards and secret agents everywhere. He was forced to hang around the park all day in a suit two sizes too small.

'You're Ed.'

'That's right.'

Prince Charles stood right in front of him.

'Camera fellow.'

'Him too.'

'Your friend?'

'Yes sir.'

'How much?'

'Twenty five.'

'Not bad.'

'Good value.'

'Busy?'

'Heaving.'

'Super.'

You had to hand it to the Prince. He certainly did his research.

Three hours later, after all the press and the photographers had been shepherded away, me and Ed were sitting on a bench outside the hospitality tent when a bloke in Reservoir Dogs shades came over. He sat down and took out an ID card. It showed a picture of a bloke wearing shades.

'We need you to stay behind for a bit tonight boys.'

'Oh yeah?'

Ed was moody. He'd missed his chance to sell the pile-up to *Wales Today* and now he was drowning his sorrows with a scotch.

'The Sheik wants to jump,' said the bloke. 'He also wants a vid.'

Ed swallowed the last of his scotch and crushed the plastic cup.

'The young Prince wanted a go too,' said the bloke, 'but we couldn't allow it. He's having a right royal sulk at the moment.'

The corner of his mouth curled up. It was probably his idea of a smile. He reached for something in the inside pocket of his jacket. Ed and I caught a glimpse of a shoulder holster and the butt of a pistol. We looked at each other.

You obviously didn't mess with this bloke.

What he took out was a brown envelope.

He placed it on the table.

'Open it.'

I opened it.

Inside there was five hundred quid in cashpoint-crisp tenners.

'Yours,' said the bloke. 'I take it we're sorted?'

'Yeah,' I said, 'sorted.'

'Good. Come with me.'

Our camera gear had been taken out of the night storage room and set up in its usual place on the podium. This was fifty yards away from the bunjee crane.

'We took the liberty,' said the bloke.

He took out his walkie-talkie and spoke to another bloke in shades who appeared out of a bush in the distance.

The whole place was empty.

No punters. No screams.

Nothing.

Then I looked down and saw Prince Charles. He was in shirtsleeves and wearing a pair of Ray-Bans. Prince William followed, his head bowed and his hands in his pockets. He kicked a paper cup that was lying about on the ground and Prince Charles told him off. Ed, noticing that the bloke in shades was still using the walkie-talkie, switched on the camera and started recording. He turned to me and winked. I began to feel uncomfortable.

Prince Charles and Prince William were joined by Kevin Spray, the local MP, and a crop of other VIPs. There was no sign of the Sheik but, when I looked up, I saw that he was already on top of the bunjee crane. He was being kitted up for the jump by three of the Canadians. I suddenly remembered how pissed they'd been when I'd last spoken to them at the hospitality tent. That made me feel even more uncomfortable.

The bloke in shades swung round.

'Is everything set?'

Ed panned quickly from Prince Charles to the Sheik.

'Fine,' he said, with an unconvincing smile.

The bloke stared at him before turning around and giving the thumbs up to the bloke in the bush. The bloke in the bush gave the thumbs up to a bloke in a raincoat. The bloke in the raincoat spoke into his lapel and, a few seconds later, a bloke with a machine gun came up to Prince Charles and whispered something in his ear before stepping back and giving the thumbs up to a bloke at the top of the crane. The bloke at the top of the crane gave the thumbs up to the bloke who was standing next to Ed.

'Okay son,' he said, 'start rolling.'

The camera had been rolling for at least three minutes but Ed wasn't going to tell him that. He gave an elaborate thumbs up sign. The bloke didn't think it was funny.

The Sheik stepped up to the jumping platform. He was waving his arms about like a fool. I gripped the wooden rail of the podium.

This was going to go wrong.

I must have seen the tape hundreds of times.

The Sheik swallow dives off the crane without any sign of hesitation. If you watch in slow-motion you can see that he's grinning. It's as if he's tasting freedom for the first time after years of bodyguards, food-tasters, servants, and full time grovellers. He's flying, arms outstretched, like a mobile crucifix. With the right kind of music, Clannad or something, it could look beautiful. At the proper speed though, it's all over in a flash.

He dives. He flies. He hits the ground like a sack.

When he bounces up from the impact his head is the wrong way round and his brain is hanging from a nearby tree.

Things get blurry for a bit as Ed zooms in and blokes appear from everywhere.

'Oh fucking hell!!'

That's the one next to us. His voice is distorted. When

CNN showed it they bleeped him out. The last thing we see is a superb shot of Prince Charles taking off his Ray-Bans. There's blood all over his shirt and he's pushed out of frame by the bloke with the machine gun.

That's it.

Twenty five seconds.

Twenty five seconds which *The Sunday Times* described as 'the most remarkable piece of visual documentation since the Zapruder footage'.

For me though, the most remarkable thing was that it was ever seen at all. I stood at the front of the podium next to the bloke. He was screaming into his walkie-talkie. Down below there was scrum of blokes around the Sheik's body. One bloke was trying to get the brain down from the tree with a stick. Suddenly the bloke standing next to me swings around. He sees Ed gone.

'Where is he?!'

'What?'

'Don't fucking mess with me pal!'

He whips out the pistol and presses it into my ear.

'Where's your mate?! Where that tape?!'

'I don't know!'

He's got me in an arm lock and I feel as if I'm going to snap. He lets go.

He checks the camera.

The tape is missing.

'Shit!'

He kicks the tripod over.

'Shit! Shit! SHIT!!'

He wipes his brow with the back of his hand. Then he presses a red button on his walkie-talkie.

'Reg, seal the area. I don't want anyone leaving the park. Do you understand?! Fucking *no-one!!*'

He comes over to me and presses the pistol to my forehead. I hear a loud click.

'You're dead meat... *boyo!!*'

I get a warm feeling and I realize I've wet myself.

★

Ed got away. In the confusion he took the tape out of the camera and made a dash for the nearest exit. No one stopped him.

Outside the park there was a row of taxis waiting to take the catering staff home. Ed hopped into the first in line and, when the driver objected, Ed gave him a hundred quid in tenners.

'Porthcawl. *Now!!*'

Nobody would dream of looking for him there.

He rented a room in a B&B and phoned ITN. He told them what he had and what he needed. God knows how they understood him. ITN took the number. At first they thought he was a nutter but when they found out about the security blackout at the park they realized something was up and they got back on the phone pronto. They sent a car from London and Ed was whisked away.

He arrived at ITN. He showed them the tape.

They were stunned.

They wanted it.

The cheque book came out.

'A hundred grand.'

Ed shook his head.

'A hundred and fifty grand.'

Ed shook his head.

'Two hundred grand.'

Ed shook his head.

'Okay, a quarter of a million but it's our final offer.'

Ed shook his head.

They couldn't believe it.

'Look son, what the hell do you want?'

Ed sat back in his chair with smile.

'A job.'

The newspapers loved it.

SHEIK SHRIEKS IN HORROR said *The Mirror*.

SHORT SHARP SHEIK SHOCK said *The Sun*.

The Times even featured an editorial calling for the immediate banning of bunjee jumps. All the papers featured stills from the video.

Ed had been clever. He'd taken a hundred grand in cash, a job as a trainee cameraman, and a royalty deal. Considering that an edited version of the tape was shown all over the world during the days that followed Ed must have become a millionaire in less than a week.

I was questioned by MI5.

They took me to a big house somewhere in Surrey and interrogated me for three days. They didn't seem to know why they were doing this. I suppose it was a face saving exercise.

In the end they drove me back to Wales in a Jag and placed an agent in the flat for a fortnight just in case Ed tried to make contact. The agent was as confused as me. He reckoned that his bosses simply wanted to duff Ed up for making them look like prats. Both of us agreed that Ed hadn't done anything illegal.

The agent's name was Roger and he said he'd once looked after Salman Rushdie. We got on well. He loved my mum's lemon spongecake and he took down the recipe for his wife. Sometimes we went for a pint in *The Flying Fox* and he even did a spot of babysitting for my sister. When he got his orders to leave my dad drove him to the station and we all shook hands on the platform. I asked him for his address in London and he presented me with his card. It said *Roger Mills. Painter & Decorator.*

Security apparently.

Prince William was taken out of Eton for a term and sent to a farm in New Zealand. No-one from the Royal Family commented on the Sheik's death. Everyone expected the Queen to say something during her Christmas Message but she didn't. She just said it had been a good year for the Commonwealth.

★

I moved out of the flat above the Rediffusion showroom and went back to live with my parents.

One day I received a letter with a Turkish stamp on it. Inside there was a brief note. It said 'Old Mill'. It was from Ed.

I went to the Old Mill and knocked on the door. Perry appeared. He'd lived there for as long as I could remember. When Ed and me had been kids he'd often taken us inside for some of his homemade raspberry squash.

'Oh hello,' he said, 'there's letter here for you.'

I opened it.

'Not bad news I hope?'

'No,' I said, 'it's okay.'

Inside there were ten post-dated cheques amounting to a quarter of a million pounds.

I opened ten separate accounts and paid in my cheques at monthly intervals. I don't know why I did this but it seemed sensible. I didn't tell anyone about the money and the only withdrawal so far has been a cheque for five thousand pounds which I sent to my uncle. I told him we were now quits.

I never saw Ed again.

I did get a phone call though. It was about a year after the events at the park.

'It's me.'

'Hi.'

'You okay?'

'Yeah.'

'The letter?'

'Yeah, I got it. Thanks.'

There was an uncomfortable pause.

'Ed, where are you?'

'Kosovo.'

'Is it good?'

'Yeah, great.'

There was another pause.

'Must dash,' he said.

'Ed?'

'Yeah?'

'Are you happy now?'

'Yes, I'm really happy.'
I smiled.
It was the longest sentence he'd ever said.

Pamela Johnson

Wig Night

Thursday's wig night.

I was flattered to be asked, but how could I go? Thursday's been wig night for eighteen years. People get used to things. She knew that.

She's a regular and there she was, that particular Thursday, delivering her best blonde bob. It wasn't all she gave me. The invitation was formal, copperplate printing with my name handwritten.

'You must come Joyce,' she said.

I'd never seen her so excited.

'You've got four weeks to sort things out, people won't mind a Wednesday for once.'

That was a month ago.

We go back a long way, me and Mrs Myerson, but it's professional not social. She was one of my first; terrified people would find out.

Privacy's everything in this job.

'Can you do it so no-one can tell?' She'd brought photos. 'Like this except for the fringe,' she said. 'I suppose I've got to have a fringe now.'

She'd been fitted up well, bought the best, very like her own. I got it closer. She'd gone to bed with a full head, woke up next day with nothing. Three small children and her husband big in the law. They did a lot of entertaining. She was devastated. That's rare. It's usually more gradual.

It would have hurt her feelings to refuse on the spot. She said I was to think about it, but I needed to put it out of my mind. It doesn't do to fret when I'm working. I left the invitation on the hall table. As soon as she'd gone I started early to calm myself. I took my time, sorted the synthetics from the real thing. They need different handling. Hundred percent human needs a proper lather, a proper shampoo. The acrylics don't need the attention, it's more like washing a garment. If I've a full house I put a few acrylics through a cold wool cycle. It's risky. There's some won't stand it, the cheaper ones. You learn from experience. No tumble dry, of course. Too much static. I didn't need the machine that night, I was ahead of myself trying not to think about what was on the hall table.

Most of mine are alopecias like Mrs Myerson. There's the orthodox Jewish ladies, and a few cancer patients. There's others look on it as a glamour item or some just can't stand their own hair, like Mrs Hawkins; her natural's got the texture of a Brillo pad. But it's mostly alopecias. Funny disease. Nobody talks about it. They can grow a baby in a test tube but they can't make your hair grow back once it's gone. Men expect it, but it devastates a woman. It's on the increase. Stress. Supermarkets can do it to you, I reckon. You never get your shopping on the belt before they start. No matter how quick you go they always finish before you. The rhythm is all wrong. I need to get my rhythm right. You can't do a job well if you don't find your own pace.

I was stop/start all that evening. Well, it must be twenty years since I've been to anything like that. She's invited all sorts.

Dinner and dance at the Savoy. She doesn't look fifty.

It's not held her back. She's got courage has Mrs Myerson and time for everyone. Committees. She does a lot of committee work, something important at Citizens Advice.

It's their silver wedding too. Funny to have got married on your birthday. 'Joyce,' she said, 'but for you, we might not have lasted twenty-five years.' Shame it's fallen on a Thursday. She must understand that it's out of the question, too many depend on it.

Once the washing was done I squeezed each one in a fresh towel; gentle, no rubbing. I need them lightly damp. Next, I eased them on to the heads. I've got six of them, wooden, on a workbench in the box room, my 'salon' is how I think of it. Bill rigged it up.

'I need them clamped,' I said. 'I need a rigid head.' So he

bolted them on. I had two dozen regulars by then.

'Joyce,' he said, 'I think you could make a go of this business.' We both knew I'd never work up West again, and I couldn't settle at Sheila's on the broadway.

He found the mirror. It makes the place.

'Close your eyes,' he said, leading me out to his pick-up.

'It looks like something from the ladies powder room at the Gaumont,' I said. He was well pleased with himself – six-foot wide with a pink tint, bevelled edges and a bluebird engraved in the corner. He always bought me a packet of Bluebird toffee for the feature film. He screwed it to the wall. I can see all six heads at once. Twelve is the most I can take, any more and I'm not giving the service. Shampoo one, roll up another, finish off a third. There's a pattern. My skill is with the rollers and the teasing out. My ladies get as long as they need on the styling.

When I first started at Raymonde's up West it was all glamour. Ingrid Bergman was my favourite. Up or down, it was always soft. Bill and me used to go to the cinema once a week, I'd buy *Picturegoer*, threepence every Thursday. 'Threepence well spent,' Bill used to say. It had photos of the stars. I studied the hairstyles. I'm good at carrying things in my head. The shape of the face is how you do it. They didn't need to look like Ingrid Bergman but if they had, say, a similar jawline then you could get away with it. I kept up with them all: Ginger Rogers, Doris Day, Jean Simmons. The only one I didn't like was Barbara Stanwyck. She had a hard face. Her hair was too tight. A good set could last the week if they used a net at night.

I was in demand, one of Raymonde's top stylists. Then suddenly, it's all cut-and-blow-dry. Angles. They wanted wedges. No rollers. And loud music. They said it gave the place *ambience*. I knew they were doing it to make you work quicker. Forty-five minutes per client – maximum – and you weren't to keep anyone waiting. It's not natural. I like peace when I'm working, I need to concentrate.

'What sort of music will she have?' I said it out loud; that happens sometimes when I'm working, I like to talk to my ladies. A band would be expensive. But then Mrs Myerson always buys hundred percent human, bespoke; first sign of root tangle and it's out.

It would have been better if she hadn't asked me. Thursday's when there's the demand. They want them back for the weekend. I collect some myself, though most deliver. Some come as far as Hampstead. I can only collect local with my problem. Even if I could shift things to the Wednesday, I'd never get as far as the Savoy.

It started after Raymonde let me go. 'I'm letting you go, Joyce,' he said. If I went up West on my own I felt sure I'd lose myself, never get back. Since Bill's gone it's got worse, even local. There's a tightening round my head till I think my skull must crack if I take another step. It's as if there's an invisible barrier I mustn't cross. There's a name for it. Long word. Can't remember. I've told no one. There's no one to tell.

I'm all right if it's not far. I put up what I call my 'handrails'. Not real of course, but that's how I think of them. Things I can hold on to. Familiar things. I've got definite routes for getting to essentials: shops, Post Office, bank, library. Anything new and I have to work out a route.

The Savoy from here – it's too far.

Some won't be able to do a Wednesday and there's some turn up without a booking, like Mrs Dallat: doesn't come for ages then, 'Just passing can you squeeze me in?' She says she doesn't wear it much; she does. You can always tell – root tangle. It's the body heat. I want to say: 'Mrs D what garment would you wear for six weeks next to your skin without washing?' But that would be unprofessional.

And what would I wear to a do like that?

It's full evening dress. I'd have to look right. Even though I don't go out much I like to look decent. I suppose it would still fit. I haven't looked at it since his sister packed it away when she cleared his clothes.

He'd planned it all, didn't tell me what it was, just said: 'We're going up West.' Must have saved for months. Black doesn't date. It was the first one I tried on. I've always liked a scalloped neckline but it was the jet beading that made it. He bought me silver shoes and matching bag. It didn't seem like twenty-five years.

'Our silver years,' he said. 'Now we're going for gold.'

He died two days before.

He'd booked a table at the Strand Palace. He even booked a car with a driver. I was going to have my hair swept up. A French pleat with bubble curls on top. I wanted to do justice to that neckline. It's important to get the hair right for the clothes. With new clients I always do it on their head once. Everyone's got their own style, it's like fingerprints. If they want something new I see them Mondays or Tuesdays, I do my shopping on Wednesdays. It would throw out the whole week.

Still, I was curious now. I wanted to try it on. Once I'd combed out the last six, up I went. I felt funny about the dress, so I found the shoes and bag first. They were in a suitcase on top of the wardrobe. I could still get away with the shoes. You can with slim ankles. I've been lucky. Encouraged, I reached for the box. It was tied up with blue ribbon that had a line of white swans along it. Swan and Edgar, Piccadilly. We had tea at Fortnums afterwards. Twelve years it's been in that box. My figure doesn't change; if anything, I've lost a bit. I thought it might have disintegrated and all I'd find would be a heap of black dust. It looked brand new, best quality *crêpe de Chine,* you can tell by the smell.

I went into the salon to get a good look in the big mirror. I took a brush to my hair. I'm grey now; used to be raven with auburn highlights. The natural wave is still there. I could do a French pleat. I'll need combs. Something with marcasite or pearls, maybe. I turned to get a look at the back.

That's when I noticed them watching me. My ladies, six of them in a row.

'It's time you did something frivolous.' It was Mrs Dallat that started them off. 'We'll manage for once Joyce.' She was encouraging.

'You deserve it.' Mrs Hawkins was backing her up.

'Just tell her you're coming.' Mrs Naylor's always been

direct. Mrs Myerson's blonde bob was full, shiny; didn't say anything, waited. Patient.

She arrived earlier than I expected the next morning. I found myself telling her about the dress. She took it to mean I was accepting. I should have told her straight away. I meant to ring her later to explain the misunderstanding, but it got harder the longer I left it.

The following week she didn't come, they were away. It was two weeks before I saw her. I was in a state. It was out of the question. I burst into tears, told her about my problem, how I couldn't get there, it was too far.

She said I should have talked to her long ago. She knows someone who could help. She had the right word for it too.

'You must come,' she said and offered to book a taxi both ways.

She was determined I was going.

'It's very kind of you Mrs Myerson,' I said, 'but perhaps it's best if I don't.'

'Joyce,' she had her hand on my arm, 'I *need* you there.'

I knew there was more to it.

Apparently it had started a month ago. A few feathery wisps at first and now it was even all over her head, about half an inch long. She took off her scarf.

'See?'

It was darker. She'd been a strawberry blonde. That happens sometimes, comes back another colour. This was to be a triple celebration, but only she and I knew about the third thing. She's not even telling Mr Myerson till she's got more to show.

'Joyce,' she said, 'I need you to help me celebrate.'

That was two weeks ago. She came round this morning. I did her here, set it on her head.

'Another couple of months and you won't be needing me,' I said.

'You can do the real thing can't you?' She looked worried. 'I won't let anyone else but you near me.'

It's funny sitting here at this time on a Thursday doing nothing. The taxi's booked for seven. It's a quarter to. I hope this French pleat holds. It's been a while since I've done anything this fancy for myself.

Untitled Monochrome Blue

He turns to leave. What is he doing here, anyway?

Its blueness tugs at him, pulls him back.

Again, he tries to leave, walks around the gallery, looks at the other exhibits; he can't help it.

Back he goes.

He sits on the white block that does for a seat; marooned in an expanse of pale wooden floor.

The canvas is vivid blue.

There is nothing but an immense blue the size of a cinema screen.

This is not his sort of exhibition, he would have said. Before. Concepts and raw pigment. 'Simply gestures,' he might have said, in another life. 'What about composition, colour, allegory. There are rules to be obeyed,' he would have argued, early on.

So why has he come?

To get out of the rain; to fill an hour between meetings; because the leaping female figure on the poster caught his eye. A blue nude beckoned.

Because she might come.

Someone joins him. He will not look. Not yet. Even so he knows it isn't her. He turns to check, sees a skinny girl in black; too young with her stick legs stretching from her short skirt to her tough black boots. Eyes lowered he sees another pair of legs moving quickly; a flash of fishnet tights, red dancing shoes, the sort she might wear. He wouldn't need to see her. He would feel her energy, catch the smell of her perfume, hear her laugh.

He turns his gaze back to the blue canvas, suspended on the white wall. He stares, wishing he didn't have to. He gets up, walks towards it, the sound of his shoes hollow on the boards. He reads the label. *Dry pigment on synthetic resin on canvas on wood, private collection*; and the statement by the artist: *This is a proposition, an indefinable, immaterial poetic event.*

It's dangerous.

An expanse of colour free from the tyranny of the line, free from any single narrative. Pigment fixed so that each grain has a life of its own, free to vibrate the purity of ultramarine.

It's a space to inhabit, a glimpse of eternity.

She would say: 'How does it make you feel? Go on, look. What do you see?'

The windscreen stretched wide on a desert night. Arizona. That's how far they would have to go. America. The other side of the world, an ocean away. If he'd dared.

The dark moment before the film begins. They went to matinees all through December. Afterwards, a cappuccino or a glass of wine and talking, talking. Her laughing. Her red hair brushing her shoulders. Late, he would take a taxi back to the office to sign cheques and letters. She would ride the bus to her studio on the river.

Blue as the nightmare he can't quite remember; she's turning her back on the tidal wave.

The colour of confession. *Bless me Father for I have sinned.*

The colour he saw the one time he kissed her. His tongue searching her mouth, the noise in her throat.

The void he wouldn't jump into. *The children, they are so young.*

Blue as his passion, stretched tight as the canvas; like the particles of pigment, caught on its surface, he's barely holding on.

Paul Lenehan

Great Bus Journeys of Dublin

Lynch had been making notes a long time with a view to making public his private thoughts on the Great Bus Journeys of Dublin, for the same reason that a literary critic might publish a slim volume of sestinas, or a mathematician might produce a paper employing only Euclidean geometry to prove the existence of God: to delight his contemporaries. To qualify as a Great Bus Journey, Lynch had first decided that the candidate should contain, within the environs which marked out its course, those contrasts of scene and expectation which a route such as the 17 exemplified. The 17 began by the blocks of flats near Rialto but ended in Blackrock, by the sea, by the old outdoor baths, the middle of whose diving boards had provided him, nineteen years before, his friends' faces bobbing in the pool below, with the first stern test of his adolescence.

He had cycled to the sea in those days with those same friends he saw no more, and had often walked his bike home when sufficient air had escaped from the mysterious slow punctures which were a feature of his youth. The 17 then was just that blur of noise that passed him by at Clonskeagh, or went sailing down Merrion Avenue with its passengers in steerage, a full cargo of parents either single or doubled, complete with progeny, beach-towels, sun-block, spades and buckets, and often a perplexed nun, who had boarded in good faith at Fosters Avenue. Now it was the contrasts which delighted him most: the hard sharp streets at one terminus, versus the houses with tennis courts at the other; the tiny tattered balconies fluttering with Monday's washing, versus a window which overlooked a cupola and the obedient sea.

Contrast, then, was the first criterion he had decided upon when assessing the credentials of a route. And yet, a bus such as the 46A, which departed early from grimy Ormond Quay and chugged brutally up the dull dual-carriageway before meandering through a succession of equally-indifferent housing developments, such a bus displayed to Lynch such a remorseless consistency of intention as to be considered almost heroic. And it too finished by the sea, in Dun Laoghaire, where the ferry waited obsequiously for emigrants, and for gleeful students of English returning to Europe, and, more than once, for Lynch himself. So it was that he concluded that the necessary condition for election to the pantheon was for the journey to contain some personal significance for the traveller – that diving-board, the gawping ferry.

And if the greatness of a bus journey was to do with its particular resonance, then Lynch knew the 75 was disqualified for sure, because he was sitting on it for the very first time. And wearing a suit, which too was rare. He was the only passenger on the upper deck, and was happy enough to accept that distinction on a February morning not yet bright enough to camouflage the cold. The bus choked its way to the top of a rise, where, away in the distance, Lynch saw an industrial estate laid out below like a scale model. That was his destination, so he fixed his tie. As the bus swung through the first in a selection of roundabouts, he tied his shoes for a second time, tied the laces tight across each instep, and the pressure served to concentrate his mind.

Lynch had earned himself an interview for the position of Clerical Administrator at a firm which distributed car tyres from a warehouse in the industrial estate, and whose small office found itself with a pressing need for such a functionary, and had advertised in all the papers for same. His initial application having met with a positive response, Lynch had investigated his slanted wardrobe, re-discovered his faithful suit, and resuscitated the cloth with a wire-brush. And thus he found himself making his debut voyage on the 75, boarding the bus like a corporate raider, his cheeks chapped from too-vigorous a shaving, which made him look much younger – no bad thing all things considered, he considered, as the bus chugged on.

Lynch had worked before, of course, in the bright headquarters of a computer firm, but that was different. He wasn't much more than a school-leaver then, with a decent set of results, anxious for the respectability imparted once a young man has chosen his career-path for the next half-a-century. Lynch had pushed paper around his desk in an open-plan office, and, as the years passed, he had got to push more significant items, but always he was pushing. Often liking to think for himself, he surmised that there might be more to life, and hence took advantage of the opportunity to take leave-of-absence for twelve months in order to travel.

This he did, living in Durban where he worked for months off the back of a truck, and near Brisbane, where he often slept in a teepee, but eventually returning home, riddled with doubt that, after all, there might be less to life than his earlier calculations had led him to believe. Such doubts in time made him mope too much, and compelled him to negotiate a part-time contract with his employers which they eagerly agreed to, for they knew by then that the management-potential of the boy who had come to them years before with marvellous acne was minimal. Thirteen months after his return from another hemisphere, Lynch handed in his resignation, having saved enough money to live for awhile; because the decision to opt out was entirely his own, his parents felt it only right that they should be disappointed in him at the time, and to reserve the right to feel let down in perpetuity.

That there was no place bleaker than an industrial estate in February was a preposition Lynch knew would be difficult to disprove. Frozen trees lined the bare drives, and the huge warehouses, lacking windows, resembled stippled nuclear-silos. People left buses and ran from the wind, and vanished through yellow doors in the sides of buildings. Lynch decided, irrespective of personal significance, that any bus which entered an industrial estate was eliminated from contention. For how could such a bus compare with for instance the glorious 33, which, once it had shaken off the debilitating influence of the city, headed for the Big Tree at Swords, and then became almost silly, weaving a carefree path first to Lusk and then hugging the coast into Rush, and thence to Skerries, (where his family had holidayed many years before in a hired caravan), the odyssey finishing at last in Balbriggan, where the ecstatic traveller, after compulsory debriefing, could purchase candy-floss from a booth.

The 75 meanwhile slid into an oil-slick by a lump of broken pavement, braked hard, and stopped close enough for the time being to the terminus, a raw outpost where a nurse in a cardigan smoked a cigarette. Lynch found the warehouse easily enough, beside a great bank of soil, on top of which an earth-mover rested like a robot-sentry. Unseen, from behind this bank, he heard a sound like a pick hitting rock, a lonely type of noise. He envisioned a muffled-up man left behind to keep up the appearance of industry, of progress, hitting out uselessly at the hard earth as per instructions. Lynch sheltered by that huge sculpted heap of soil and smoked a cigarette. Two taut birds jeered from a shivering tree. Lynch scuffed the welt of his shiny shoe against a slab, and the noise was sufficient to startle them into flight. They spun round for a time, then headed over the bank, over the earth-mover, and away. He killed the cigarette and dropped a pair of mints into his mouth.

A Mr. Walsh and a Mr. Higgins received him at the warehouse, and bade him seat himself in a dull little room into which daylight entered only by accident through an air vent. A sore yellow glow shone in its stead from filaments on each wall, and shone on the scarred table where the Messrs. Walsh and Higgins sat side-by-side, and where Lynch sat dutifully opposite. The two men began by poring with intent over his staunch C.V.

'Twenty-eight, are you?' Mr Walsh abruptly inquired, as if by accident.

Lynch agreed that he had reached that landmark, and his response tallied with the information given on his C.V; and, although in real life he was not so very far away from his thirty-third birthday and looked it each morning just on waking, he took a nervous delight in the knowledge that there was not a lot the Messrs. Higgins and Walsh could do right that minute no matter what age or nationality or political persuasion or gender he might declare himself to be.

'There are some gaps here, you know,' Mr. Higgins then decided, pointing with his finger at the opened page.

'Yes, there are gaps alright,' Mr Walsh harmonised.

Lynch felt that first cold lick of fear in his throat, like the desperation felt by an examinee with two full questions to answer as the invigilator announces a mere ten minutes remaining in which to get a life.

'I wanted to experience different cultures, different ethnic traditions and social systems, to broaden my mind and to give myself a more expansive world-view, do you know what I mean?'

The Messrs. Higgins and Walsh stared hard at him, the former nodding minutely, the latter not. Lynch sat his ground and awaited their next move.

'Yes,' said Mr. Higgins, 'there may be some value in what you say. But, you haven't worked much, have you, in the last good while?'

'I've been unlucky,' Lynch revealed. 'I know the economy has picked up, and that's good news for us all, but, to be frank, vacancies in my area have been few and far between. Believe me, I've tried, I've tried hard.'

This last assertion was patently untrue, Lynch knew it as he watched his interviewers turn to the next page of his hardy C.V. For a number of years now he had been content just to survive, and to claim all time as his own. If he fancied a coffee he drank a coffee on the mezzanine level of a mall, or read a book on a bench, or just stretched out on the floor of his room and listened for tremors. He lived life in fact just like the rich man, but without the hard currency, which is where in the long run his system had let him down, and led him instead to a room without daylight to answer so many questions.

And then, only twenty minutes after making his windswept entrance Lynch discovered that the compulsory winding-down of the interview had already been reached, and Mr Higgins was asking: 'But why do you think you might be suitable for this job?' Lynch, having worked all those years in

Admin. for the computer firm, knew that a highly-motivated child could be trained in less than a month to carry out the duties of a Clerical Administrator. Instead, he talked about the importance of his experience in a similar position some years before, about his determination to resume his rightful place in the workforce, and about the commitment he already felt to the Messrs. Higgins and Walsh and their impressive warehouse of tyres.

Why he wanted the job, of course, was because the starting rate which it offered would provide him, even after tax, with almost twice the money the dole offered, and now he needed money more; to save for the course on hypnotherapy which he coveted, to replace his ill-fitting collection of garments, and to finance his rediscovered sex drive, which had absented itself during his darkest days, but now, again fit and firm, had directed itself at the woman with red-hair who supervised the launderette, and who handled his basket of briefs with a gentle eroticism which staggered him sideways.

He was allowed to expound upon the importance of staff loyalty for just a little longer before papers were shuffled, glances exchanged, and Mr. Higgins, in time-honoured fashion, applied the finishing touch.

'Is there anything you'd like to... eh, ask us at all?'

'The bus, the 75,' Lynch inquired, having prepared his question earlier that morning, 'is that the only service into the estate?'

This practical inquiry seemed to baffle his interlocutors, for they ceased shuffling paper and sat quite still.

'Is there a more interesting route, I'm just wondering?' Lynch continued, in their silence.

Mr. Higgins took a fountain-pen from his breast-pocket, unscrewed the cap to no avail, replaced it, returned the pen to his pocket, and nodded, while Mr. Walsh watched intently as his colleague performed his manoeuvre.

'I'm not quite sure what...?' offered Mr. Higgins.

'Don't you like it?' Mr. Walsh inquired.

'Well, frankly, no,' Lynch decided, offering a smile to show his possession of a vibrant sense of humour, so necessary if everyone in the work-place was to pull together for the greater good. 'I mean, it's hardly one of the Great Bus Journeys of Dublin, am I right?'

'I drive, myself,' Mr. Higgins was moved enough eventually to reveal.

'We both do,' Mr. Walsh added. 'Why don't you ask at a depot?'

This good advice concluded the interview. Lynch shook hands with both men, who both wished him all the best in the future irrespective of what might happen there, which was more than kind.

Outside, at reception, two gangling youths waited in grey suits, and their eyes searched Lynch for clues as he passed. 'See you next Monday,' he called to the receptionist, and strode away. At the bus shelter he lit a cigarette, less in celebration than to salute the possible – it was still possible that no eighteen-year old with a stutter would apply for a job for which he or she was vastly overqualified; it was still possible that those ample gaps in his C.V. would be viewed as signifying an enviable flexibility of approach rather than proof that the perpetrator was guilty of treason against the institutions of the state. The more he thought about his interview, the less distressed he felt – even when the 75 arrived, and he faced the prospect of that dull journey back. He took the top deck again, and the bus lurched away, and rain began to fall on the corrugated roofs, and men in dungarees huddled beneath awnings.

Because it was still early, and the rain looked like easing, he decided to return home, collect the wedge and putter, and connect up with the 44B to Glencullen, where a golf ball could be hacked around a windy pitch 'n' putt course on top of the mountain. Due to sharing much of its route with the fabulous 44, which began at Burgh Quay and ended thirteen miles away in pastoral Enniskerry, in an entirely different county, the Glencullen bus was debarred from contention as a Great Bus Journey, in the same way that the number 1 was debarred due to the brevity of its route, allied to the fact that it left its terminus only twice each day and never on a Sunday, and was therefore regarded as non-existent by many, or legendary at least, the unicorn of buses. With the industrial estate far behind, and a heater blowing warmth around his ankles, and the prospect to come of shanks, slices, and many misread putts, Lynch felt nearer to bliss. He closed his eyes, opened them in time to see a light change to red. He lay down on the back seat with his legs curled, and when he tried to open his eyes again, they refused, and the bus rocked him gently, warmly, as it went on its way.

When he awoke, the 75 stood quite still on a ragged stretch of lane with a few cottages alongside one kerb only. The rain, as he had foreseen, had drifted, and the same weak sun shone one more time. He went downstairs to investigate and found every other passenger had gone, vanished, along with the driver. No-one had thought to check the seats for sleeping men, and so there he was, becalmed in an unknown lay-by. An orange triangle parked behind the bus signalled a mechanical failure of some description. In one direction the lane widened, like a tar river, and Lynch headed towards its mouth. The noise of traffic sounded almost suddenly, as if a switch had been flicked, and increased in volume as he walked towards its source. And there, at the end of the lay-by, he could see that the main road was not far away. Across a strip of rough land, a wire fence marked the border with the carriageway. It presented itself as a simple operation, merely to cross the scrub-patch and climb a fence whose height was not daunting for a man pretending to be twenty-eight. Lynch, instead, sat down on a ridge in the full glare of the bright cold sun.

His formal clothes felt less awkward on him then, and his leather shoes had ceased to pinch so persistently. He felt more tranquil somehow as the cars flung past him, thundering madly over the rumble-strips, so urgent, so necessary, all those lives careering past with the same sun flashing for a moment off every windscreen, as if the occupants had been chosen. Extraordinary, he knew, to feel so suddenly content, with the noise of the motorway soothing him now like the pulse of a steady breath, the hard brightness all around him as if he too might be chosen for some purpose. He squinted hard as a single-decker powered into the distance, thought it might have been the 44B, but then the 44B never came this way – or did it, for where was he anyway, stranded in some lay-by he'd never seen before, where was he? Maybe, he wondered, maybe this was the mystical point where all the bus-routes crossed, like those sites where ley-lines meet which become shrines where people gather.

Behind him the 75 still slumbered, broken-down, awaiting repair, and the thought crossed his mind that perhaps the bus had broken down on purpose, somehow aware of his low evaluation of its route, determined to become a Great Bus Journey no matter what the cost, to make a place for itself in his memory as the bus on which he had once been abandoned. That was stupid he knew, that was so stupid it made him smile. The shouts of children came from a garden, and he heard them approach. He knew they had stopped, shocked or frightened by the strange man sitting on the edge, dressed in his best suit, so he pushed himself up, pulled a silly face for their amusement, then hurried down the hill through the bunches of weeds.

The Big Wheel

High winds stalled the ferris wheel on the last night of the funfair. The bucket-seats creaked in the gale and the metal joists strained, but the wheel remained unmoved. Too dangerous, the barkers explained, in their weary, end-of-season voices. Hilda was disappointed by the cancelled ride more for her boy than for herself. She called him Dermot. It was his birthday. He was four years old. Unlike her son, Hilda had already enjoyed the ferris wheel the week before, accompanied by the same man who flanked her child as the three followed after the disappointed throng. His name was Niall. Hilda had met him first six months before. Her son liked him, and so did she.

Hilda had left Dermot with the baby-sitter the previous week because she felt that both Niall and herself needed the space that the absence of a child creates. Her pulse that night had soared with the squeals of girls when the operator stopped their seat at the zenith of the wheel's persistent orbit. The city below had winked a million giddy lights back at her, so beautiful, so kind from a distance, all its sad stories and heartache made bearable by the magic of perspective. She'd felt suddenly wiser, like those stories of astronauts who peer back at planet Earth and understand.

Because Niall had sat beside her, cosy with his arm around her, pointing out all the landmarks he knew, she felt he might be partly responsible for such a rare impression – which made no sense, she knew. Yet she was grateful, and took it as a sign. And then, on the very night Hilda returned with Niall and her son, the ferris wheel refused to turn. So, each holding one of the boy's upraised arms, all three followed the crowd towards the giant marquee, while all around them gaudy balloons wriggled skywards and away.

Inside the marquee, metal scoops whirled screaming people round and round. A huge galleon rose slowly into the air before whooshing back towards terra firma, like a macabre experiment. The human cargo within shrieked as they surrendered to the bliss of engineering. Hilda and Dermot and Niall watched as the punters left that ride dizzy and confused, checking for the whereabouts of their stomachs and hearts. The boy's initial shock at all that noise and light had by then subsided. Niall bought him a candyfloss.

Later, Hilda sat her son in a plastic car and watched as the carousel turned at a child's pace. The boy's face slumped slowly towards the ersatz dashboard, as if the strain of showing both bewilderment and joy for his adults could not for long be sustained. All three rode the ghost-train side-by-side. Niall and Hilda joked to relieve a child's distrust of darkness. Niall rode the roller coaster on his own, while Hilda and her son watched from a viewing platform. His canted face passed her at speed, full of wonder. She liked his courage, she decided. Four weeks later, for a trial period, he moved in with Hilda and her boy.

Hilda rented a maisonette in an old-fashioned, red-bricked neighbourhood. All the ground-floor windows had capacious sills on which chatterers could rest to while away some time. Behind these houses a new shopping mall was half-built on a site where once a huge warehouse had stood. The Lone Parents cheque and Rent Allowance took care of necessities, and Hilda worked part-time in a flower shop to pay for treats. Her employer handed over cash in an envelope each Friday. Hilda asked no questions; her son's education, her video and TV – these achievements, she felt, justified such a modest transgression.

Within a week of his arrival, Niall had fixed all the domestic gizmos that hadn't whirred or spun in months. He slept on a sofa in the living room, beneath a counterpane, lulled to sleep by the warmth of a fire. Hilda admitted him into her bed only gradually, because the sheets had known only her warmth for so long. After they'd made love he would return to the couch by the fireside, until she should decide otherwise. When Hilda rose in the mornings to prepare her son for school, Niall was long gone, bedclothes stacked neatly by the stairs. He worked as a postman, returning each afternoon in his uniform like a soldier back from a skirmish. Each Friday he made his contribution towards the household costs. And each evening, before dark, he wheeled Dermot up and down the blind street on his postman's bicycle.

Hilda had feared that her son might resent that portion of her affection which she took from him to give to the new man in their life. Instead, Dermot responded with a child's uncluttered intuition. She felt that her son enjoyed the new dimension to their home life – the more interesting shape of the triangle as opposed to the unvarying line. He never thought of Niall as his Daddy, she observed, and never called him such. But then 'Daddy' might not be her son's favourite word. 'Daddy' for him meant absence, tears, hurt, voices far louder than required. And each time she remembered the boy's father, the man she'd left two years before with her eyes red and her hopes skewered, each time she remembered she twisted the skin on her arm to remind her to forget.

She didn't hate him, she couldn't hate him; because she'd lived with him and loved him and borne his child, she knew she would never love as intensely again. Love dies, she felt, but its soul lives on in stashed photographs, in the texture of daylight one afternoon in a garden, in the unspoken question sometimes visible in the eyes of her boy. An envelope with a London postmark arrived from her ex each early September, in time for his son's birthday, with some sterling notes within for the boy, and a scrawled note that wished her well. There would never be reconciliation, Hilda knew – lightning strikes twice only if you never learn. Yet she was attracted to the idea of starting again, and of someone new. Niall meanwhile continued to roam the house with a toolbox, correcting cupboards and shelves.

Then, in late November, Dermot's atopic asthma worsened for no reason his mother could explain. Hilda kept the house as free as possible from dust, and feather pillows, from any allergens that might menace him. But for two nights running, just before bedtime, a coughing jag shook the boy's thin frame. Hilda took him to the bathroom where he spat out the mucus his swollen bronchia had made. Then she tucked him up in bed. She told Niall not to worry, that her son's intermittent asthma subsided after days, and was not heard from again for months. But after a three-day respite, the boy spat again into the wash-hand basin while his anxious mother watched.

His manner changed; where once her son had been good-natured, now he became sullen. The supervisor of the Montessori where Hilda left him two mornings a week told her that Dermot's smile had disappeared. Had anything altered in his domestic situation, the supervisor wondered? That evening Dermot took his crayons and drew a pair of eyes upon a sheet of paper-green eyes, huge, with coal-black pupils staring from each socket. Hilda woke one night to the sound of her son calling. When she ran to him he had calmly resumed his sleep. Niall smiled in sympathy when she re-emerged from the room. He had heard all the shouting, he explained. She told him to go back downstairs.

Next morning she took her son to the park. A night's rain had churned the grass into a muddy mess. Bundles of leaves hugged the nets on the unused tennis courts. Hilda and Dermot kept to the cinder path. Dermot took no interest in the evidence of November – the hockey shouts from a hidden field, the hiss of traffic on wet roadways, the delight of unleashed dogs eluding their owners. Hilda took her boy to a bench on the perimeter. They watched the frothy water in the flooded weir. Hilda took his face in her hands and turned his eyes to her own. Was Niall always kind, she asked. Was Niall always good? Dermot's four-year old eyes looked back with a mannequin's eerie blankness. Where was her son, Hilda wondered? Who had taken him from her?

That night a strange sound startled her awake. She lay in the heavy darkness and listened with each pore of her skin. She heard her own quickened breath, and from her son's room she heard... nothing. A swathe of light illuminated the landing outside her half-open door. She tiptoed to the threshold and peeked out. She saw Niall flush the toilet on the stairwell, and heard the cistern respond with a series of glottal caws. She watched him hawk a ball of phlegm from his throat and drop it quietly into the bowl. He took a chunk of toilet paper from the roll and wiped the rim of the bowl clean. He'd done nothing strange, yet to Hilda he felt like a stranger. She crept back to bed and lay awake and listened.

The next morning Niall called on Hilda at the florist's shop. He smiled as she let lilacs fall, although she could no longer recognise his smile. Was it a smile, she wondered; what did it signify? Niall demanded to know why their relationship had so abruptly cooled. Hilda shrugged, made him tea in the back room. She talked to him through a hatch while she dressed a bouquet. Did she want him to go, he wondered. He agreed to leave her life if he no longer made her happy. His openness made Hilda feel suddenly absurd. She remembered the good-naturedness which had first attracted her. She remembered the funfair that first time, that sense of miraculous suspension as the ferris wheel span through the sky. She gave him a hyacinth, a blue hyacinth, for Constancy.

Dermot's lethargy disappeared. Hilda delighted again in his vitality, the sheen that returned to his eyes. He laughed once more when Niall wheeled him down the street on the crossbar. At the Montessori school the supervisor noted an improvement in the boy's demeanour. She talked to Hilda of the phases children go through, of the unnecessary worry parents must endure. In the park Dermot clambered up knolls and revelled in the mud. Snow fell briefly in December while they walked through the illuminated streets. Two weeks before Christmas, Dermot took a jotter from his holdall in the hallway. With his pencil he drew the same harsh eyes as before. The boyish light which had shone from within was extinguished again.

Two nights later Hilda laid her boy in bed and kissed him goodnight. At the door she stopped, arrested by his small cry of pain. She watched him knead his stomach, then turn onto his back. She examined him with stalled breath but found no signs of hurt. Who owned the eyes she asked, but he said nothing. She shushed him to sleep with mothers' words. Niall was waiting on the landing when she emerged from the bedroom. He offered her his palms in a gesture of bewilderment. The half-light hid his face. Hilda only saw his eyes glitter. Into her mind came the image of a pike, peering out from murky water. She started to cry. Niall climbed towards her, but her face hardened. He shook his head and smiled again that peculiar smile. He walked downstairs to his makeshift bed.

Hilda rose the next morning just as Niall secured the front door behind him. From the window she watched him pedal his bike in the direction of the sorting office some miles away. She roused her son and dressed him quickly. Dermot's stoic face showed no animation. Hilda dropped him off early at school and hurried home. In the living room she bundled all Niall's belongings into refuse sacks. His worldly goods made no impressive display. A few clothes and shoes, an electric shaver, a mandolin which rarely yielded tunes to his leaden fingers, a 'HOW IT WORKS' parts 1 and 2, all the drills and bits and braces which fitted snugly into each compartment of his tool-box. She knew he had no letters amongst his possessions for she had previously inventoried his worldly goods, out of curiosity. Niall kept no record of his past. He had no history.

She hauled both refuse sacks into the street and left them by the farther sill. Then she returned inside and waited. Niall rounded the far corner just after two, his gawky thighs almost perpendicular to the bicycle frame. Halfway to her door he saw the refuse sacks and slowed. He clambered down and examined their contents. Crouched behind the front door, Hilda heard the discord as he replaced the mandolin on top of a pile of his belongings. She heard him tap-tap-tap on the window, once, twice, three times, like a Morse message passed between prisoners in adjacent cells. She heard a squeak as the flap of the letterbox lifted. His eyes were above her, staring into her privacy. She heard him breathe softly outside her door. The flap banged shut and shocked her. He tied the refuse sacks together and hung the arrangement round his neck. She watched from the window as he scooted away, straining with each thrust of the pedal to keep his world upright. He roared at a car that took the corner at speed. He looked back only once. Then he lurched away.

Christmas distracted the mother and child. There was a non-shedding tree to buy, and presents to choose, and happy films to watch on TV. Dermot only rarely asked after Niall, and Hilda was glad. They enjoyed dinner at her mother's house on Christmas Day. When they returned home in the evening, their street was dense with snow. When Hilda turned the key in the front door, she felt a premonition of strangeness from somewhere within. She approached each room reluctantly. One hand held the hand of her sleepy child, the other flung open each door and rushed for the light-switch. Nothing, no-one, and yet, something had altered.

She put her son in bed and covered him with quilts. Behind the houses, snow had frozen white on the scaffolding and gantries of the unfinished mall. Hilda from the frosted window saw the jagged outline of a moon base, barren, deserted, its occupants dissolved into powder by an alien atmosphere. She drew the curtains tight and left her son to sleep. In the kitchen, making cocoa, she sensed a faint tang of urine, a stale unmistakable smell. She stopped on each step of the stairs, afraid, waiting for a footfall or a whisper. She left the door of her room open wide, and tried hard not to sleep. Weariness made her eyelids droop, the dark tempted her to rest. Snow, snow made the world so quiet.

Her eyes opened into blackness. What had woken her? She heard the noise of murmuring, like the eerie sound monks make at plainchant. Because she understood the geography of the house, she approached her son's room in darkness, step by slow step. The murmuring continued in a small voice, her son's voice, a soft babbling sound that stalled her breath. She eased his door open by degrees, and crouched down on the threshold, and skinned her eyes into the interior. A whisper of snowy whiteness backlit the curtained window. Her son continued his incoherent gurgling, the speech of the half-sleeper.

From his bed two green eyes stared back at Hilda's frozen face. The thorn-black pupils grew rounder as she softly approached. She moved closer. She knew. A cat, a wild cat, one of the many strays driven from its refuge when work on the new mall had begun. The cat rested placidly on her son's stomach. Emboldened by fear, her hands gripped its coarse neck and she ran with the snarling bundle down the stairs. She flung the spitting cat into the white night. It pawed over the snow slowly, as if used to rejection. Upstairs her son had quietened. His calm face showed no sign of trauma. Hilda crawled into the bed beside him and held him close. She hoped he would ignore her speeding heart.

Dermot's sleep was troubled no further by the prowler who had for so long provoked his wheezy breathing. Hilda secured the loose wainscot in the scullery herself, with a hammer and nails. Niall had talked once of fixing it, but, what with his work and other chores, had never got round to it. He wrote to her twice in January, from his new address. Hilda declined to reply. It wasn't his fault, she knew it wasn't his fault, yet she would always associate him with that period of anxiety and fear.

In September another letter from London arrived. Hilda handed the card and money to her son, and watched while he scrutinised each banknote. Now we can go back to the big wheel, he said, despite not having once mentioned the funfair, nor the stalled ride, since the disappointment of last year's birthday. More and more his face resembled the face of his father.

Malcolm Lewis

The Dream of David Lloyd George

In 1917, in the campaign for Palestine, the 53rd (Welsh)
Infantry Division, without artillery support, several times
advanced on Turkish placements at Gaza, suffering terrible
loss.

That rare searing summer
the fig's thin hands spread beside his door
on green rickety arms,
its roots tip-toe in the old well
under the Cricieth house.

It vexes him, under the walls.
Cut to the ground
its milk sap clots black on the doorstep.

It grows back.
Knuckles punch upward through the floor.
A dry green sea rises;
five-fingered hands pluck him from his bed,
fine white hair trailing.

He feels himself passed along Arab streets
(the crowds spit, turn their backs)
to Lloyd George Street and the fat Turkey fig
outside Jerusalem railway station.
He's dropped flat, arms out like Jesus Christ.

An Arab woman
he'd once hardly noticed
crosslegged on a Cardiff pavement
nods to the first man,
a Welch Fusilier, filthy with wounds,

and Dafy,
who marched him into Turkish guns
to have Jerusalem for the Empire's Christmas gift,
knows the sin and feels
a studded boot press on him.

Five thousand Gazan ghosts
walk over him –
one step small recompense.

After them, a tubercular man
who came from Fflint to the sun,
a Liberal for Home Rule,
a cobbler, an honest Baptist,
and an Arab now, with a wife and child.

He steps and presses on the proud head
and Dafy's under, sucking the dry soil
with the roots and the once-believing dead.

Whisper

Her whisper grows
carries behind watchful eyes
where comrades go

tended in simple rooms
passed on in field, factory
kitchen, yard

shyly grows
feels through the soil
around the prison walls

snares cables
taps transmitters
proliferates, cannot be stifled

until, its time come,
it appears in the streets
and twists and swells through the city:

it overruns fences
cleaves doors;
it penetrates hidden rooms

fingers handcuffs, wires,
iron beds,
lists of names.

It pollinates telephones.
And turns to the light,
exults, whorls,

frisks in daylight
in the rambling open city
unfurling garden of trumpets, flags, drums.

★

A breeze in the streets and fields.
She checks in the mirror
her best cotton dress, her hair,
puts on her broad-brimmed hat.

She calls her grand-daughter.
In the early sun, hand in hand
bright as washed fruit
they walk out with the people.

Toilet

I kept his mouth moist –
spoonfed him water,
wiped away lip-froth with cotton buds,
but dehydrated, he still pissed.
It woke him, and he grunted 'toilet'.
I lifted the bed sheets
and him, light as a child.

I cradled him on the commode,
pulled down his winceyette pyjamas,
manoeuvred his legs apart.
My eyes looked anywhere
but at his dick and chicken-skin scrotum,
obscenely normal between skin-sagged legs;
his eyes though were always closed.

Comrade

The unused parlour – lino floor,
glass cabinet with tea set and Lenin bust,
the writing desk he'd made himself
for the Branch records and minute books –
was always cold, never a fire there,
except then, for that old man
lying in the bed brought downstairs,
his flesh starved, his unweighted spine
stretched like a cosmonaut's in space,
the fire's heat sucking the clean cold under the door.

Settee

Through the tunnel Dewi's airgun pellet gouged in the
        frosted pane,
John Bevan, calling at the back door, saw Dewi's parents
        fuck
on that stained fake-leather settee –
so close to the fireplace the side was cracked and peeling
        off –
there where the kids played, battering it, collapsing the
        springs and stuffing,
scrambling and hanging on their car, stagecoach,
        castle, mountain,
and where their father joined in, excited too –
him, a child still, a clean and pressed boy,
and where, rampant out of his clothes, he lay on his own
        children —
then Dewi smashing John for telling other boys,
Dewi kneeing him in the bollocks, kicking, eye-poking him,
and old Mr Meredith, coming home from work, grabbing
        his ear,
dragging him away for fighting dirty,
calling him a coward, a little cunt.

Mo McAuley

Sorting Out the Ponies

An African sun hangs over an Accrington field. Mary Ann squints against the glare, climbs over the garden fence and drops down into the grass next to the ponies.

She picks up a twig and pokes it through the hole in the concrete post that carries the middle wire of the fence. Shocked brown earwigs tumble from their lair and scuttle away like scorpions into the long grass. Mary Ann shudders with satisfaction then unties the ponies and sets off for the stable: Mino, the Palamino, is like a gilded fairground pony; Beauty, a black mare with a white diamond on her forehead.

Crickets whir deep within the yellowed grass and fat bees murmur as they caress the clover beneath their bodies. Across the field, the ducks quack raucously, their laughter carrying from the pond that lies in a hollow near the neighbouring fence. Mary Ann walks the ponies over the crazy-paving bed of the dried up stream, up the hill and into their stable. She chats to them as she opens her grooming box and takes out a metal curry comb.

'What you doing, talking to them brushes?'

Billy Snalem stands watching her at the open door of the shed, his eyes huge and gleaming behind the jam jar lens of his glasses, the frames of which are held together with pink elastoplast. Mary Ann stops, frozen in her tracks, her mother's old hair comb hovering over the bristles of the tall brush. The other brush leans against the shelf, its head buried into a string shopping bag, stuffed tight with dried grass.

Billy is ten and a half years old; Mary Ann is just nine. His worn, grey shorts are always wedged up his behind where he's been scratching himself and he often has nits. His mother spends most of her time in the pub, his father most of his time in prison. No-one is allowed to play with Billy so he hangs about, watching others.

'Why you talking to them brushes?' he repeats. 'And don't say you wasn't 'cause I've been watching.'

His gaze wanders around the shed, to the loops of bias binding sewn together and attached at strategic points with small safety pins – the head collars. Two old dog leads hang on the nails beside them – the lead reins. A cardboard box sits on the floor, full of scrubbing brushes and dusters; elastic bands for plaiting manes and tails; two faded pieces of satin-edged blanket, the names of each pony sewn in chain stitch across the corners.

Billy puts a toe over the threshold and pokes the fresh grass newly scattered on the floor. The old pile is heaped tidily behind the back of the shed. Mary Ann feels afraid. He will tell everyone in the playground about her game. The only time anyone listens to Billy is when he's telling tales or making things up to get attention – about Father Christmas not being real, about the noises in the bedroom when his Dad's away, about Mary Ann talking to brushes in the shed.

She looks at the brushes, now so obviously only brushes, propped up on the shelf together. One has a ribbon tied in among the bristles, the other a splodge of white paint in the middle of its head – a white diamond. In the corners of the window there are furry, grey-white bundles of spider nests. The surrounding webs hold the shining wings of flies and the crooked legs of daddy-long-legs abandoned in a desperate bid for escape. She hasn't noticed this before.

'It's just a game,' she says at last, her voice small and shaky.

Billy's courage grows at her defensiveness. He steps into the shed, setting the floor boards creaking underfoot, and stalks around like a detective. He moves towards the two brushes.

'Leave them alone, Billy! Mum's in the kitchen. I'll yell for her, I will.'

Billy smiles, revealing large, gappy front teeth.

'She dunt frighten me. I'm not frightened of anybody, me. Any road....' He reaches out a nail bitten hand, letting it hover near the brush and watching Mary Ann's reaction. 'I'll get me own Mum round. She'll sort your Mum out. Everyone's scared of me Mum,' he adds proudly.

Anger rises in Mary Ann. The back of her neck begins to prickle, a sure sign of temper. She scratches hard at the nape of her neck.

'Get out Billy, go on, bugger off.'

'You swore! I'll tell on you. Your mum dunt like that sort of thing. Your mum thinks she's posh, better than rest round here. You're mental you are, talking to brushes like that.' Billy pushes his lower lip out with his tongue and points a finger to his temple, making a screwing action to emphasise the point.

Suddenly he grabs a brush and runs out of the shed. He straddles the pole and pretends to gallop around the field. Tears start in Mary Ann's eyes. Beauty, he's taken Beauty.

Billy jumps an imaginary fence, laughing at the pretence. 'I'll take it t'Grand National,' he shouts and heads off in the direction of the duck pond. Mary Ann chases after him, brushing the tears away with one hand while the other still tries to scratch the red hot angry neck.

Mosquito larvae thrash in the retreating water of the pond. Plump, white Aylesbury ducks sit among the mess of droppings and mud. Billy edges down the bank, sending the flies up into a whirling frenzy around his head. Behind the fence, the neighbouring geese sway their necks and hiss.

'Want some water, horsey?' Billy holds the head of the brush down to the stagnant water. He dips the bristles in, making sure they get duck shit on their tips. Mary Ann watches from above. Suddenly she rushes down the bank with a banshee cry. She grabs the brush and wrestles with the pole. At first Billy laughs as they struggle but Mary Ann's stick-like arms are stiff and strong with anger. She wrests the brush from his hand, holds it high in the air then whacks him across the head with it. At the same time, she raises a leg and kicks the boy back into the pond as hard as she can. Billy lands on his back in the turbid water. His glasses have slipped from his eyes and lie halfway down his cheeks, smeared with dirt. He fumbles to stretch the bendy wire behind his ears. Mary Ann holds tight to the brush and runs.

The kitchen window is fogged with condensation; Mary Ann's mother is doing the weekly wash and making lemon curd at the same time. The earthenware jar rattles inside the pan of bubbling water.

Mary Ann suddenly appears at the back door, out of breath and obviously out of sorts. Her mother looks up in surprise. Mary Ann twists one leg behind the other, hiding a new graze on her dirty knee. She has managed to avoid a bath two nights running.

Her mother carries on hauling a wet sheet from the washing machine and feeds it through the rollers of the mangle. The mangle slowly spews out the sheet, stiff and squashed into a flat, creased package. Mary Ann stays in the doorway, silent and watching, scratching the back of her neck.

'What's the matter? Have you been up to mischief?' her mother asks.

'No!'

Mary Ann kicks a sandalled toe at the doorframe and looks down at the floor.

'Are you frightened of Billy Snalem's mum?' she asks at last.

Mary Ann's mother laughs. 'What a funny thing to say! I don't know the woman and from what I've heard I don't want to either. I'm not keen on you mixing with young Billy, I'll admit, although we should be kind to those worse off than us.' She adds dutifully, 'It's not Billy's fault after all.'

'I hate Billy Snalem. I wish he were dead.'

'Well, that's not very nice is it? And it's was not were.'

'I don't care. In fact, he might be dead already. And good riddance to bad rubbish.'

She is pleased with this dramatic statement and her use of 'in fact'. But her mother doesn't respond and Mary Ann is changing her mind about mentioning the duck pond incident.

Her mother's hands are puffy and red with water and detergent. They skilfully guide the clothes through the mangle. Mary Ann's and her sister's small knickers are gathered together in a bundle with bigger items so they won't become lodged and go round and round the rollers. They emerge on the other side, packed tight in the folds of another flattened sheet.

'Can I put something through?' Mary Ann asks this every holiday wash day and each time is refused. She never gives up.

'It's too dangerous. You'll get your fingers trapped. Remember what happened to Susan....' Her mother launches into the familiar cautionary tale of trapped fingers, broken and bleeding in the rollers of the mangle. Mary Ann is only allowed to put the powder in, shaking the blue granules onto the clothes, pressing the button to set the prop revolving, backwards and forwards, swishing through the water and churning the clothes. She likes to watch the granules dissolve in the hot water, the bubbles begin to form. But she is old enough now to do more.

'Am I too old for pretend?' she asks. Her mother laughs.

'Of course not, no-one's ever too old for pretend.'

Mary Ann knows this isn't true. Her mother doesn't play horses with brushes or make teepees with dried, rosebay willow herb stalks. She cooks and bakes and sews and washes and cleans.

'It's good to use your imagination. But I would like some of my kitchen back from your horse game,' her mother says. 'I could do with the string bag for a while, until I get round to buying a new one.'

'You can have it all back. I don't want them any more.'

Her mother glances across but Mary Ann looks away from her eyes. She picks up the peg bag. Her mother lifts the heavy wicker basket of washing. They go out into the garden to the line. Some of the pegs have faces painted on their round wooden heads, strands of wool for hair and scraps of fabric for dresses and shawls. The peg family live a gypsies' life. They have a caravan which is colourful and patterned with huge, spoked wheels, painted red and yellow. Mary Ann hands pegs to her mother who holds one in the corner of her mouth while she deals with another.

'I bet there's no such thing as Father Christmas,' Mary Ann's heart pounds as she says this, a statement rather than a question.

Her mother stops in surprise and takes the peg from her mouth.

'Goodness, what brought that up in the middle of August?'

'In fact, I know there's no Father Christmas. It's just you and Dad, isn't it? I saw the presents under your bed.'

Her mother finishes the sheet she is looping along the line and puts up the prop to stop it draping on the dusty, dry garden. Mary Ann feels her discomfort and wishes she didn't. She wants to bury her head in the flowery pinafore and take back what she has just said. But this time she can't.

Her mother kneels down. Her face is level with Mary Ann's. Her arms encircle the small frame.

'You've had a lot of fun out of it over the years, haven't you? All the excitement of waiting for Father Christmas, leaving him mince pies and the carrots for the reindeer.' Her eyes seem to beg forgiveness. Mary Ann feels sick in the stomach. She shrugs and pulls a face.

'It doesn't matter. I'm not bothered or anything. So you bought me that cowgirl outfit?'

Her mother nods.

'And the selection boxes and the slippers and nightie. And the cash register?' Her mother still nods.

The sun beats down on the washing. A breeze buffets the sheets and sets the socks and pants dancing on the line. The prop sways a little.

'Perfect drying weather,' her mother comments and Mary Ann agrees. They walk back toward the house, Mary Ann carrying the peg bag, her mother with the washing basket under her arm, resting it on her hip. The brush lies on the ground across the path.

'That's dangerous there,' her mother says. She notes the white paint daubed on the head of the brush. 'Better take Beauty back to the stable, keep her out of trouble.'

'It's Pal who causes....' Embarrassment creeps over Mary Ann. She picks up the brush and leans it against the outhouse wall.

Billy Snalem is waiting by the kitchen door. Mary Ann's

mother straightens up tall to face the unexpected situation. Mary Ann's heart beats hard and fast.

'Hello Billy, what brings you here, looking all dishevelled?' her mother says. Her voice sounds strange, too jolly and friendly. Her mouth is set in a smile.

'She pushed me in the pond. She whacked me, she did, right across here with that brush,' Billy points to the side of his head and to the brush leaning against the wall. 'It's lucky I'm not dead, or gone daft or something.'

Mary Ann feels her mother's tension. She sucks in her bottom lip and looks down at the ground.

'Is that true Mary Ann? Did you hit Billy with the brush?'

'He picked on me first. He was laughing at me.'

'That's not really the point is it. Did you hit him with the brush?'

'Yes.'

Billy smirks and scratches himself.

'Then you'd better apologise right now. I won't put up with that kind of behaviour. I can't believe you did such a thing. Go on, say you're sorry.'

Mary Ann mumbles an apology. Her mother makes her repeat it, louder and clearer and in a more heartfelt fashion.

Billy smiles cheerfully.

'I told me own Mum. She told me to sod off and sort it out. She says I just make things up.'

Mary Ann glances up at her mother, curious to see her reaction to this. Her mouth remains fixed in a smile and her voice is still jolly when she speaks.

'Oh well, it's sorted now. Would you like me to look at your head for you?'

Billy looks surprised, then pleased, then embarrassed.

'No, no I'm alright really.' He puts his hands in his pockets. 'Right, I'll be off then.' He crosses the garden and climbs the fence into the field.

Mary Ann sits in her bedroom, being punished. She kneels up on her bed and looks out of the window across the fields and allotments, beyond the rows of terraced houses toward the

118

Pennines. A train snakes its way across the viaduct and slides into a tunnel in the hillside. She counts the seconds until it reappears and makes up a story about lost trains disappearing into mountains, full of wailing, ghostly passengers. Her stomach rumbles from lack of food.

'Can we make a cake?' she asks in the kitchen later that day. 'Jenny Shuttleworth's mum lets her do baking.'

'I don't see why not,' her mother replies. 'You're very responsible these days. Most of the time anyway,' she adds with a wry look. 'We can use the lemon curd I made. It should be cool enough by now.'

Mary Ann's chest swells with pride as she rows the eggs along the table. She carefully taps the shells on the edge of the bowl and lets the eggs slither on top of each other, her tongue gripped between her teeth as she concentrates hard. She weighs the sugar and butter and puts them to one side while she opens a new bag of flour. It thuds out of the packet into the measuring bowl, making the scales clank. Annoyed at her clumsiness, she waves away the white cloud and scoops out the excess with her hands. As she washes her hands at the sink her mind flickers back to Billy Snalem and the shed. She pulls herself up by the taps to see out of the window. The contents of the shed are scattered over the grass and the door is flapping open. Mino's head is crammed into a bucket. She returns to the table where her mother is spooning lemon curd from the earthenware pot into shiny glass jars. She questions her daughter's silence with a smile but Mary Ann blinks back the tears and carries on with her measuring. This isn't the right time to talk about it, not now, not with all this work to get done. And sorting out the ponies will just have to wait.

The Apple of His Eye

Kate removed her headphones and rubbed her eyes, defeated at last by the rolling picture and static buzz. All around her, bemused Zimbabweans still gazed at Emma Thompson tumbling over the video screen in her empire-line dress. *Sense and Sensibility* on a night bus from Hwange to Victoria Falls. What had they done to deserve this?

Outside, the sun was collapsing on the horizon and acacias had flattened into black parasols against the blood-orange sky. Inside, small sounds intensified in the dark: the rattle of ice in plastic glasses; the crackle of cellophane as hands fumbled for popcorn; the half-hearted grumble of children being settled down to sleep. Kate put back her seat and closed her eyes to enjoy the cosy, relaxing atmosphere of the bus. Immediately, the parting row with Alex was back in her mind.

It was such a shame. When they got on, they *really* got on. But when they argued... Yet the evening had started well enough, making love in the hotel bedroom when they should have been eating dinner with the rest of the crew. It was the conversation afterwards that ruined everything.

Alex had rolled angrily back onto his own pillow.

'Whatís the matter now?' Kate asked.

'The usual, that's what. We make love then you immediately distance yourself from me.'

'I just asked you not to ring or e-mail when I'm away. I know other women love all that but I find it claustrophobic. I'm not into this possessive, sentimental stuff. You know that.'

Kate had gone to the bathroom at that point. Alex had trailed after her, running his fingers through his hair in frustration, his face gaunt with tension. He had carried on talking to her through the shower curtain.

'Why do you do this to me? We've been together nearly three years yet you act like a teenager, pulling me close, then pushing me away.'

The argument lasted until she left. Alex stayed behind in the hotel room. He still doesn't know she missed the plane in the end.

The bus rumbled on into the descending dark. Kate put her seat back up into the sitting position. It was impossible to sleep with her mind sifting through the argument. Richard and Judy, Bangers and Mash, Alex and Kate. They were a 'documentary dream team' according to colleagues and everyone assumed their personal life must be similarly blissful and creative. It was more like an Australian soap these days, Kate thought sourly.

Thank goodness she was going home for a while. It would be great to see the family again and she was looking forward to taking her father out for a belated birthday meal although it would be strange at first, being back in England and in the office again. But at least this leisurely journey gave her time to adjust to the cultural changes ahead, with the help of Jane Austen.

Kate turned on her reading lamp and glanced at the old man next to her to make sure he wasn't disturbed. He looked frail when he was asleep, with his head thrown back and his mouth slightly open. His hair was snow white under the beam, his dark skin dusted grey with age. In the sagging crotch of his trousers, one hand rested inside the other, palms upwards. The skin was a pale, coral pink, crazed by dark, pencil line creases. His shirt gaped open, revealing grey-white chest hair and a sinewy neck in which a pulse beat slowly. There was a white crystalline sprinkling on the curve of one ear. Dried soap perhaps? Kate felt her chest tighten with emotion; her father always managed to leave shaving soap somewhere on his face. She felt an urge to wipe it away tenderly. Suddenly, she couldn't wait to get home.

*

They didn't talk much on the journey back from the restaurant and Kate's father made it obvious he preferred it that way.

121

He was impatient to get out of the car when they reached the house. Kate tried to help but he pushed her hand away with his walking stick.

'I manage when you're not here and I can manage now,' he said. It's been been a favourite line of his since Kate's mother died fifteen years ago. He resurrected a subject from the restaurant to distract attention from his struggle.

'You're an imbecile staying on. Mugabe's a maniac.'

'I know what I'm doing Dad. I've worked in Africa enough to judge what's what. Besides, I've got a commitment with the elephant project.'

He steadied himself, using the door as support for one arm, his walking stick the other. He would be fine in a minute, he explained, it was just that his knees stiffened up.

Kate leaned against the car and lifted her face to the sun. She closed her eyes.

'I work better when there's an edge,' she said to mid-air. 'Anyway, you used to go mad if Jamie and I gave anything up before it was finished. It's your fault I'm like this.'

She opened her eyes to see his reaction. He looked like a garden gnome with his blue eyes watering with hidden laughter and his cheeks and nose rosy-red with thread veins. He was still hanging on to the door. A wince of pain crossed his face as he tried to move away. Wary of further rebuff, Kate didn't offer to help again. They stood, frozen in obstinacy, in the driveway.

The next day, Kate paused outside her brother's Edwardian terraced house before going inside. It all looked just the same but then nothing ever changed in Dipley; not her father's clockwork routine in the crumbling family house nor Jamie's symbiotic existence with his wife.

Two standard bay trees stood guard either side of the front door, their terracotta pots chained to iron rings cemented into the wall. Each time she saw the manacled pots she was reminded of Jamie and Eleanor inside. They, like the bay trees, were a perfect matching pair, one barely distinguishable from the other these days. Pot bound.

Inside, Kate sat at the kitchen table and waited for her coffee. Above her head, the muffled voices of Eleanor and the children seeped through the tongue and groove ceiling.

At last Jamie put a quivering cappuccino in front of her. 'There!'

'Wow!' Kate said, amused by his triumphant smile.

It lit up a handsome, undemanding face which bore none of the features dominating her appearance: not a hint of their father's long, stubborn jaw or their mother's tilted nose that looked like a plastic surgery job but was entirely home-grown.

'How are the kids?'

'Fine thanks. They're desperate to hear about the animals, preferably tearing each other to pieces. Have you finished your series? You could do with getting out of there I would have thought.'

'Don't you start. I'm just relieved to get away for a while; the wrapping up stage gets a bit tense.'

'How's Alex?'

'Fine.'

'Is that all I'm getting?'

'Yep.'

Jamie's expression was suddenly serious as he placed a large manilla envelope on the table between them.

'We haven't got you for long I'm sure, so I'm going to get this over with,' he said. 'I think we might have to do something about Dad.'

'What do you mean do something?'

'You took him home yesterday, you must have seen, the door's usually wide open for burglars. The house is a complete tip but he still refuses to have any help.'

'Does it matter if he's happy? You should travel through Africa. That would put Dad's hygiene in perspective.'

Jamie didn't laugh. He pulled two shiny brochures out of the envelope. Each had pictures of smiling, elderly people on the front; men and women in perfect harmony at last, now they were in nursing homes.

'Come on, Jamie. It would kill Dad to be in an institution. He'd never leave that house and all those memories of Mum.'

She pushed her cup to one side, still half full. No more caffeine, it made her aggressive. And Jamie's coffee suddenly seemed strong and biting under the light, frothy veneer.

'But something's got to change,' he said. 'The business has been struggling and I need to earn some decent money, get myself a 'proper job' as the kids call it. And if I do that, I can't be on hand for Dad.'

He pushed the brochures towards her Each had a motif of some sort on the cover – a weeping birch drooping over a pond, a garden bench under a leafy arbour. One was for the Evergreens Nursing Home, the other for Silver Birch Retirement Flats.

'What a load of silly euphemism,' Kate said. 'What's wrong with Rotting Roots or Shrivelled Sap. Where are the bloody commodes or dentures? Why can't people get real about ageing.'

She leaned back in her chair, stubbornly viewing the brochures from afar.

Jamie leaned forward and locked his fingers.

'I know this isn't pleasant but decent homes have waiting lists. It's no good sticking our heads in the sand until something terrible happens. He's only had a mild stroke but that often precedes something serious.'

He got up to find the sugar bowl. Kate stared across at his empty chair. A mild stroke. He's had a mild stroke. Why has no one told her? She shouldn't be shocked by the news of course. He's always smoked too many cigars and drunk like the proverbial fish and he's been overweight and suffered from high blood pressure for years. And he's always been selfish; selfish enough to die without telling her. She loves him. She hates him. She's always loved and hated him. But mainly loved him. The bastard.

She remembered their outings on Saturday mornings to collect his weekly supply of whisky and cigars, and sweets for Jamie and herself. It was their little ritual and she always looked forward to it. She squatted down next to him to look through the glass front of the counter while he updated Mr. Currie on her latest escapades. His shoes gleamed like conkers and the smell of polish was pungent in her nostrils. He was fussy about his shoes and she always helped him to clean them, using a wooden cocktail stick to poke polish from the holes that looped around in lacey patterns.

Each anecdote ended with a caution but the tone was always indulgent and accompanied by a sly wink in Mr. Currie's direction. The contradictory messages confused and angered her sometimes: exhortation one minute, reproval the next, often for the same exploit. His moods were unpredictable and his will was strong, like hers. It was the foundation of their relationship. He saw her as a 'character' in the same mould as himself, and she lived up to expectation. Jamie's role wasn't so exciting: sensible and steady in work and play, that was all he wanted to be. Or perhaps all he was allowed to be, the thought struck Kate as she slid the brochures back into the envelope.

'You should have told me,' she said.

'He didn't want you to know. He didn't want to disrupt your work.'

Kate didn't reply.

'You were always the apple of Dad's eye,' Jamie said as they sat in the car park of the Evergreens Nursing Home. He rested his hands on the steering wheel and looked through the windscreen.

'So that's why he never tells me anything important.'

They sat in silence for a while. The sky had turned chinchilla grey and a strong wind tossed the hanging baskets outside the nursing home like balls on a string. The new brick of the building was a raw, angry red where rain had lashed its sides. Large drops spotted fitfully on the glass as another downpour threatened. Jamie turned on the wipers to clear the windscreen.

'Well there's no way Dad's going in there,' Kate said at last.

She felt an angry heat radiate from her brother. Abruptly, he turned the engine over and swung the car round in a sharp circle.

'Easy to say when you're buggering off back to Africa,' he said, 'What happens if he has another, serious stroke? I may

125

not be around and I haven't got room at home. And you haven't got a permanent home at all. So what's the answer, one that's workable, and palatable for you?'

★

The door was open. Kate walked quietly down the corridor, past the grandfather clock with the tick she turned into tunes in her head as a child. She went into the kitchen. Bluebottles buzzed and settled on the pile of food-encrusted plates and a wasp crept around the rim of a tea cup. Kate felt a guilty affinity with their invasion. She turned to retrace her steps to the front door, to announce her official arrival.

Her father stood behind her, watching. Kate forced a smile. Suddenly she saw evidence of the stroke, not just outwardly but within. Why hadn't she noticed his decline the other day?

'*Because it suits you not to see or feel,*' Alex would say, '*Because you can only go so far in caring, or being cared for, then you back off and put up the shutters.*'

An emotional coward he had called her the night she left Zimbabwe.

Kate glanced at her father's shoes. They were dull and scuffed and the laces were frayed.

'Come and sit down a minute,' he said, surprising her.

Kate needed a few moments away from him.

'Shall I make a cup of tea first?'

'Alright. A fresh cup would be nice. But don't go on about the washing up. You know I can't stand nagging.'

They sat beside each other on the sofa. He was in good form and wanted to hear about the elephant watch project. After all, he reminded her, it was his enthusiasm for natural history that had set her on this path.

It was just like old times. Kate embellished her tales with jokes and exaggerated the dangers and hardships, while her father laughed and slapped his thighs in approval.

They discussed conservation and argued about game hunting, almost came to blows about land rights. Finally, they reminisced about holidays in Norfolk: how they had dodged the spears of marram grass rattling on the sand dunes and how they ran full pelt down onto the beach, where the wind whipped their legs and stole their voices away. And they remembered digging their heels into the hard wet ribs of sand and the feel of binoculars bumping against their chests as they strolled toward the wading birds in the shallows. They talked about everything except the real issue.

As they slowly walked down the corridor Kate realised she hadn't mentioned the Golden Panda nomination for her last series on Madagascar. Suddenly she didn't want him to know.

At the door, they stood and looked at each other – old mates, sparring partners, fellow adventurers. Kate lingered but it was obvious he'd had enough. He held her hand and squeezed it in a farewell gesture.

Kate kissed his cheek and left the house.

The phone line to Zimbabwe was clearer than on a domestic call.

'Is everything okay?' Alex asked.

'Yeah. It was a good meeting. I've checked something out by the way; there's an opportunity for me to work back here, if I want to.'

'Not that you do, I suppose. But I'm not asking about the meeting. I just wondered why you were ringing again. That's twice this week. Is the family okay?'

'Oh, there's a few changes and problems but nothing insurmountable.'

'You're not checking up on me then I hope. You know I find it claustrophobic.'

'Ha ha.' Kate hesitated. 'Actually, it's not all that fine. Have you a minute? I won't keep you long, I don't need your help or anything...'

'I'm listening, I *want* to help. Get on with it woman!'

★

Kate's hands overflowed with flowers and scissors, a trowel and a fork. She pushed open the oak gate with her hip and walked up the gravel path towards the cemetery. At the top of the hill, she looked out over the dales. Tracks of dry-stone wall dissected the green expanse into neat little boxes, each containing a cluster of sheep, like a child's farmyard set. A heat haze hovered in the distance and vapour trails plummeted from a sky that was clear blue apart from the odd smear of cirrus cloud. Bees squirmed in the flowers on the graves and a woodpigeon called softly from the canopy of a copper beech.

The sounds and colours of the English countryside were so soothing after Africa. Her senses had become accustomed to atonal cries and bloodcurdling shrieks, vast tracts of red-brown earth broken up by spurts of garish colour. Africa was an impressionistic riot compared to this wispy, watercolour of an English landscape. Insipid she would have called it not long ago. And now?

Her mother's grave had been tended but not for a while, Kate was pleased to see. She pulled out weeds and wiped away dirt from the gold lettering on the plaque. It was set into a large sandstone rock which was rough and uneven and pleasingly natural. A moat of gravel surrounded it. She trimmed the grass edges with a pair of scissors then plucked out the stray tufts from the stones before smoothing them out with the flat of her hand.

Finally, she filled the canister with fresh water and flowers and kneeled back to admire her work.

'Maria Hampton. Born 17th February 1929. Died 6th July 1985. *'Her heart was full of love, her body full of warmth, her mind full of ideas. She was my life.'*

Her father had written those words and Kate had been overwhelmed by the strength of emotion, his certainty in his love. He was devastated when his wife died, sitting by the body, stroking her hand and fingering the thinned-gold band of her wedding ring. He kissed her face like a young lover, then rested his head on her chest and cried and cried. Kate's own anguish remained silent, like a dry, rough hank of muslin choking her throat. It was as if the strength of his passion sapped and diminished hers, turning her into a bystander rather than a daughter who had lost her mother.

The price of love is often pain, the minister said at the funeral as Jamie and Kate stood either side of their father in the church. And Kate had silently vowed, 'I don't ever want to pay that price again.'

She glanced around. There was only a woman and her young child at the far end of the cemetery. She bent down and kissed her mother's name, and cried.

*

The bus noisily dropped a gear as it approached the village. Kate jolted awake and sat up quickly in her seat, forgetting for a moment that she was back in Africa. Next to her, a little girl straddled her sleeping mother's lap and sucked her thumb. She lifted her head to scratch the tight black braids of hair running like miniature train tracks over her scalp, then flopped back onto her mother's chest. A shy smile crept around the wet thumb. Kate winked and smiled back.

She felt a childish twinge of excitement. She had asked Alex to catch the bus from Hwange and meet her at the Victoria Falls terminus, with a change of clothes and a tie.

'I've become addicted to buses driving through African sunsets, I want you to experience it too. Do you think I'm mad?'

Nothing about her behaviour surprised him, he said. He was beyond surprises. I hope not, Kate had almost replied. Her father had a good win on the horses before she left and given her a share, on the understanding that she spent it in a frivolous manner. She had booked a weekend in the vulgar, colonial splendour of the Victoria Falls Hotel.

The bus turned into a dusty main street awash with fluorescent light from tatty souvenir shops and travel bureaux. The terminus was next to a burger bar. The bus stopped. Through the window, Kate spotted Alex in the doorway, bundled up in a cream jumper and denim jacket against the cold African night. His sun-bleached hair stood up in wayward tufts around his head and he was wearing his usual faded black jeans and desert boots. It would take more than a tie to make him look presentable; he always looked like he'd just got out of bed. He was searching for money in his pockets as begging children clustered around his legs. He gave out fistfuls of dollars and coins. More children appeared as if by magic. He looked flustered as he rummaged about his clothing for more and produced a couple of chocolate bars as well. Alex was always a magnet for beggars wherever they went; he had never managed to toughen up and keep them at a distance. She felt a surge of affection and desire for him.

The door hissed open.

Alex watched and waited as she approached. He looked apprehensive but pleased to see her. Kate dropped her bag at their feet and smiled up at him.

'Good journey?' she asked.

'Novel. A Jane Austen novel on video can you believe. *Sense and Sensibility.*'

Kate giggled. 'I wondered if you'd get that. I had *Emma* this time. The bus company must have bought a job lot. Do you think this is an omen? We really should be heading home.'

'It depends doesn't it? How's it left with your Dad?'

'He's agreed to have help with his meals and the house. We're going to review the rest.'

She put up her arms. Alex encircled her with his. She felt the roughness of his jumper on her face.

'I've missed you such a lot,' she said.

'I know, all those e-mails and phone calls... drove me crazy.'

Kate play-punched him in the back.

'I just needed to talk to you about Dad, this nursing home business, about me working back home. I needed...' She struggled to finish the sentence.

'Me?'

'Okay then, *you*!' She grabbed his arm. 'Come on, I've got a treat for you.'

They walked away from the shops and across the dusty street, dodging the battered cars and taxis, down into the bush that lined the road. 'But first,' she said, 'you have to pass a test.'

'Oh God, haven't I been tested enough over the years.'

'Only a simple one. Tell me, and be dead straight with me, am I the apple of your eye?'

'That's a funny old phrase.'

Alex stopped next to the bulbous trunk of a baobab tree. He ran his hands over the bark where animals had rubbed it shiny and smooth. He frowned as he stroked and appeared to be thinking hard.

'No, you're not, you're a bloody thorn in my side. But I love you all the same. So that's real love, isn't it?'

They stood quietly together. Across the road, a family of baboons strutted along the grass verge, the youngsters stopping now and then to tussle until an adult male irritably gave them a clout. Nearby, a nervy flock of guinea fowl set up a clamour and scurried away into the undergrowth. Stars glittered on a black velvet sky. Kate linked arms with Alex and steered him in the direction of the hotel.

Maria McCann

Jacob enlists in the New Model Army

(Extract from a novel)

The sun grew stronger on my face. Noon. My head ached as from strong drink and I wished only to remain lying and speak to none. A woman passed me with a little child, walking by on the other side. Afterwards I tried to rise, but getting upon my feet my body pitched forwards and I was again stretched in the dust. I rolled onto my back. The walnut was in my throat, burning the flesh black, but I could lose it by falling asleep. The old man stood over me, dropping something onto my face. I said to him, *They are in bed at the inn together, but he is dead of the fever*; I made to sit upright but my head was nailed to the ground. He forced another nut between my teeth, a hard one. It let something cold into my mouth.

'Keep your feet on him,' a man said. I could feel no feet on my body; was someone standing on me? There was a smell of smoke and I heard our horses run into the wood.

The sky was wet. I lay on my back and saw men move at the sides of my head before darkness closed over me again.

'His eyes opened,' said a gentle voice near me, and then, 'drink.' The hard thing was once more put between my lips and I turned my head away.

'Leave him, Ferris.'

'We cannot leave him like this.' Warm fingers wiped my mouth and chin. I looked up to see a young man gazing perplexed into the distance, his profile lean and pensive, but full-lipped and long-nosed. He knelt at my side as if watching for someone, his hand still absently stroking my lips so that I breathed its scent of sweat and gunmetal.

I coughed against his palm, and he turned on me a pair of

eyes as grey as my own. Pale hair hung thick on his collar; I
saw he had shaved some days before. As I met his eyes they
darkened, the pupils opening out like drops of black ink fallen
into the grey, then he looked away, and his fingers slid from
my face.

'Let me drink,' I creaked out.

'Get on your side.' He tugged at my arm, gritting his teeth
as he tried to roll me over. 'Up. Up on your elbow.' When he
had pulled me into position, I reached out my hand for the
water, and caught a wry look from him.

'You could have saved me a job. Here, and don't spill, this
is precious.'

There was mould on the sleeve of his jacket. I took the
metal flask, swallowed about half, and handed it back.

He waved his hand. 'Drink more,' and he stayed close as if
to say, *I don't go until you do.*

I sat up and looked about me for the other man I had
heard, but he was gone. On both sides of the road, pressed
around small fires, were soldiers wrapped in garments that
had once been bright red but now were faded to yellow or
filthied to shades of brown, except where patches had escaped
the mud and smoke of battle. At one fire nearby a boy sat
watching us. He smiled and beckoned to my new-found
friend.

'We got some water down you earlier. Drink anyway. I'll
fetch you some victual.' Ferris sprang up and walked off,
stopping to speak with the lad I had noticed and clap him on
the shoulder before passing behind a group of men and out
of my sight. Pale blue smoke blew across me, smelling of
home, and a thin rain, like spit between the teeth, chilled my
neck. I could see now the cropped hair of the young boys
round the fires. Some of them, and most of the older men,
still wore theirs long. I put my hand up to my head; someone
had cut my hair close to the scalp. There it lay on the grass,
a knot of wet black vipers.

'Feel better?' He was back, squatting easily by my side.

'Did you do this?'

Ferris glanced at the dead-man's-locks on the grass. 'No.' He held something out to me, but I could not take my eyes away from what had once been myself, and was also Izzy and Zeb.

'Here,' he pulled my hand away from my shorn skull, 'best eat without looking.' It was bread and cheese, the bread hard as your heels and the cheese popping with mites, but I grabbed at it.

'Not too fast if you haven't eaten lately, you'll hurt yourself,' said Ferris. 'Easy, easy!' He snatched the cheese from me.

'Why are you feeding me?'

'Call it your ration. You're in the New Model Army.'

'You mistake. I am –'

'We lack men. What, going to lie down and die are you?' He laughed.

'But I'm weak, unwell. I've been starving.'

'Starving!' The grey eyes mocked me. 'Granted you're somewhat hungry. We see it all the time. And that suit of clothes! We thought we'd found us a deserter, a Cavalier officer. Until you spoke.'

'I said nothing to them.'

'Oh yes. While I was bringing you round. And struggled. We stood on your coat to keep you down.' He offered me the bread and cheese again. 'Some of the lads thought we'd caught up with Rupert of the Rhine.'

'He's a devil,' I mumbled into the tough crust.

'So they said, and they were about to take a short way with you, but I told them, Prince Rupert's not a man you'd find lying in the road. What *is* your name?'

'I – well, I have a mind now to be Rupert.'

'Aye, who wouldn't be! Roast goose for him, no bread and cheese.'

'Were you told to enlist me?'

'No. I am squeamish – would not leave a man to die of thirst on the highway – so I came to see if you were well enough to enlist. You're well enough now,' and as I made to protest, 'now.' He jerked his hand towards one of the fires. 'Yonder's your corporal – he'll teach you your drill.'

I considered. 'Is it all bread and cheese?'

'Not always that good! But there's beef sometimes, and eight pence a day – when they pay it.'

He got up and put out his hand to me, but my hip-bones, dry as the ones in Ezekiel, grated as I struggled upright, so that my weight pulled him down; laughing, he was forced to leave go.

While I was lying in the road the day had passed into evening, and I was glad Ferris walked before me as it was hard to discern either form or order in the groups of soldiers lying round the fires. He stopped in front of a man whose hair was so dirty it might have been of any colour, and was soiled with more than mud: as I looked closer I saw brownish blood all down the right side of his face, cracked where the sweat had oozed up under it.

'Prince Rupert come to serve under you, Sir,' said Ferris. I bowed awkwardly. The men around laughed.

'And what might be his real name?' asked this gentleman, whose voice was pinched with pain.

'If I may, Sir,' I put in before Ferris could spoil my game, 'I will take the name Rupert, since it seems I am known by it already.'

He waved his hand as if to say, what was that to him?

I was put down in the Officer's book as Rupert Cane – the first name that came to mind – and ten shillings given into my hand.

'That's your entertainment money,' said Ferris, who was come with me.

'Entertainment?'

'Money on your first coming in. Keep tight hold, you won't see that much again.'

I was handed a red coat, two shirts, breeches, and hose; also a leather snapsack and a cap with dried blood on it, as if peeled from the head of a corpse.

'I can't get this coat on,' I said, holding it up.

The man shrugged. 'Nothing I can do there. One yard of cloth, that's the regulation.'

'Suppose you gave him two, and we got a tailor to run them together,' suggested Ferris.

135

The fellow was willing enough. I thanked him from my heart and Ferris took up the coats, saying he knew a man would undertake the work for a shilling.

As we walked across the camp I felt the food warming me and longed for more. To take my mind off it, I asked Ferris what would happen the next day.

'We will see to your coat... and you'll be drilled in the pike,' he added.

'*You* are surely not a pikeman!' I said, without thinking.

He stopped and gave me a hard look. 'I have outlived many pikemen.'

'I did not mean –' but my voice faltered, for I had meant it. There was a pike over the fireplace of the great hall at Beaurepair, and all the men had lifted it at one time or another. Ferris was of too slender a make to carry such a weapon. It might be, I thought, that he had some little thing to do, far from the van of the fighting. But carrying a pike was better than lying a corpse by the roadside, and for this I owed him thanks. I smiled on him and he at once returned the smile.

'If you would know,' he said, 'I was a musketeer. But a man that knew me in London thought I might be more use elsewhere.'

'Where – why?'

'I am not bad at the mathematics, and some of his best were just then dead. So now I help with artillery,' he said as we seated ourselves at a fire. 'Really it is for the cavalry to do, but what with fever and shot – well, they need men who can count without their fingers,' his mouth twisted at his own grim jest, 'fire straight, and dodge whatever comes back. When the enemy are in range, so are we.' He held my eyes and I felt myself rebuked.

'I know nothing of war,' I said.

'Would that I could say the same. It is a bestial occupation.'

'Yet it is said the men of this army are rather godly than beastly. Is it not the other side that plunders? Do they not call Rupert, *Duke of Plunderland*?'

Ferris grinned. 'Is that why you took his name? Aye, there

are those who sing psalms in battle, and our commanders take pains to hold in the plunderers, but not for love of the vanquished. They see rather that armies need friends, and that soldiers once run wild are insensible of authority. Especially if they chance on Popish wine.' He threw a stick into the flames. 'A man may sing psalms, you know, yet cut the defeated in shreds with as little mercy as – ' he paused for a comparison, and ended by shrugging.

Warmed by the fire, I stripped myself and tried the new shirt and breeches, Ferris watching me in silence. The shirt was coarse but almost clean; both it and the breeches were big enough. These last had pockets, a new thing for me. My old garments I put in the snapsack, but when I took off my shoes, the fine hose that Peter and my brothers had given me were worn to rags. Not without regret, I put them on the fire.

'Ferris, you said 'Especially Popish wine.' Is it so strong?'

He laughed 'Any wine a soldier finds is Popish. That salves conscience.'

I gazed at him. 'Do you say there are no goodly soldiers? That all are wolves?'

'Soldiers are but men. There are many both brave and merciful –' Ferris paused to wave in greeting as a figure skirted the fire. 'As for the other side, they are more than even with us –'

He broke off and called eagerly to the new arrival. 'Welcome my lad, and did you get any?'

I looked up and saw a boy almost as tall as myself, all legs and arms. His face shone with pleasure and even in the poor light I was struck by the gem-like brilliance of his blue eyes, the kind which often go with yellow hair. This boy's hair, however, was so dark a brown as to be almost black, and I thought I recognised the lad who had waved earlier from the fireside.

'This is Nathan,' said Ferris. 'A good comrade and *not* beastly.'

'Who called me beastly?' asked the boy. 'See, Ferris,' and without awaiting a reply he pulled a cloth from under his coat and proceeded to unwrap two chunks of roast meat, the fat gleaming in the reddish light. 'There's bread too.'

'You are a marvel,' Ferris told him. Turning to me he added, 'The meat's mostly boiled.'

'I guess this was picked up at Devizes,' the boy said.

Ferris grinned at him. 'Plunder, eh? Is there enough for Prince Rupert here?'

'Prince –?' He giggled, regarding me curiously, then said, 'I think we have not met before?'

'I joined up today.'

Nathan seated himself on the other side of Ferris and began slicing the beef with a dagger, trying to make three portions out of two. To my surprise he showed no sullenness at this unexpected reduction in rations. 'Is your name really Rupert?'

I nodded.

'You're from these parts?'

'Right again.'

'I wager you'll be pikes. They always put big fellows on pikes,' and he commenced telling me the weight of a pikeman's armour. He had altogether too much to say, and his voice grated on me.

Ferris, watching my face, said to Nathan, 'He'd bear the armour well enough, if there were any.'

'Surely,' the boy agreed. He passed the meat to Ferris and began cutting bread.

'Even I could carry what they issue now,' Ferris continued with a glance at me. 'But most men don't want it. A buffcoat – that's the thing.'

'Would you wish to be a pikeman?' Nathan asked him.

'I wager Rupert thinks me unfit for any kind of soldier.'

'O, no,' I said, 'I only –'

'And he is right,' Ferris went on. 'The recruiting officers are told to find the tallest strongest men, and what do they turn up? Seven years older than Nat, and not as tall.'

He passed me some beef and Nathan held out a piece of bread. I tasted my share and relished its very toughness as making it last longer. Ferris crammed roast flesh into his own mouth and closed his eyes, sighing as he bit into it. I watched Nathan layer his bread and meat, holding them delicately in long hands which hardly seemed fitted for soldiering.

Looking back at Ferris I found him staring at me. He said, 'For all that you think, I can put down any man my own size—'

'Nay, taller,' said Nathan.

'— and I wager that's as much as you can do.'

Nathan coughed. A morsel of bread shot out of his mouth, brilliant in the firelight, and I saw that he was laughing.

'Nat, you'll choke one of these days,' Ferris warned.

This made the boy worse. I heard great snorts as he fought to swallow his food.

'What ails him?' I asked, vexed at his silliness for I felt I was somehow being made a mock of.

'Me and my bravado. He knows I am no brawler, eh Nat?' Ferris handed me more beef. Nathan continuing to giggle, I rose, sensing myself in a false position. The two of them turned laughing faces up to me.

'Where did you get the meat?' I asked. 'I will try for some more,' and indeed I could have eaten the whole lot twice over.

'That fire over there.' Nathan pointed. 'But they won't give you any. It was a favour to me.'

'We shall see.' I made my way to the fire he had indicated and found some beef still in it, roasting on a stick. This I seized. The two whose food it was crying out in protest, I offered to fight first one then the other for it, and appealed to the others sitting around to judge if that was fair. They, being bored and ready for any diversion, said that it was. I then held myself upright and let the beef-cooks get a good look at me. 'Well,' I said, 'which of you shall be first?' and made to take off my coat. Neither budged, so I took up the meat and left them to the contemplation of their cowardice and the jeers of their companions.

Ferris and the boy were pushing one another, still laughing, when I returned with my trophy. They stopped at once upon seeing it, and Nathan gasped, 'How did you persuade them to that?'

Ferris leapt up. 'I can guess how,' he said, and he had the stick away from me before I knew it. 'I will tell them it was nothing but jest. Nat, give me this,' and picking up the cloth

139

he strolled off towards the other fire while I stood amazed, considering whether I should bloody his mouth for him, if he returned.

Return he did, cloth in hand, and after grinning at me, straightway sat down at my feet.

'What do you mean,' I said, 'by – hey, you, what do you mean?' It was awkward standing thus over a man on the ground and talking to him. Nathan glanced anxiously up at me.

'Sit here and I'll tell you.' Ferris patted the grass. I squatted next to him, my anger ready to flame out at a very little thing.

'That's the second time today I've saved your life,' he said.

'Saved my life! They were near beshitten for fear of me.'

'Can you catch musket balls in your teeth? Those men are musketeers.'

I recalled Mervyn's syllabub.

'I have told them you were in drink, meant the thing as a jest and would have brought it back, only you forgot the place,' Ferris went on. 'I suppose you are not really the Duke of Plunderland? They do say he goes about in disguise.'

Had someone at home – Zeb, or Peter – said such things, he would have smarted for it. I glared at Ferris.

He looked steadily back. 'Ah, yes. You are full as big as he. Able to put me in the ground without a weapon, eh?' He began untying the cloth. 'Are you still hungry? Are you, Nat?'

A flush spread over my cheeks.

'Here.' Ferris opened up the last folds and pushed the bundle of meat towards me. 'No bread this time.'

Nathan was full of admiration. 'Brave Ferris! Where did you get it?'

'From them, of course. I begged another share as reward for bringing it back.'

From *As Meat Loves Salt*, to be published by HarperCollins Flamingo, February 2001.

Fiona Owen

Picnic on Ajman Beach

Was the sky really red? Day sky,
    but growing plum-purple like night
so we must pack up quickly.
    A shamal is coming, Father said.
And yes, I could feel my skin
    prickling with the whipped up sand
and the bay was a bowl of water
    tipped to slopping over edges.

Sand stings with a wind at it, and my legs were bare,
so I must hop on the spot.
          Mother had her arms full
of baby boys and was heading for the car when the man
came from across the beach, his robe flapping.
          He was old,
like the Ancient Mariner, with the same beard and eyes.
Salam alaykum, he said, and Father spoke back, picking up
the ice-box and fold-up chair.
          My long hair was twirling
in the tug-chase wind, and maybe I said *Come on, Daddy.*
Then I was aware of the old man's stare and the way
his hands waved over me.
          No, no, Father laughed,
and went to go, but the fisher man grasped his arm
and told my father *camels, gold, a dhow* like a rime
with a ring to it.
          Sand was in my eyes, my ears
and I was grinding my teeth on it. The whole world
was graining into sand-storm and, somewhere in the frame
was me, smalling to a speck enough to get blown away.

141

Mother (who can't swim)

Coming up for air, I see you at the shoreline
circled by black rubber and thick glass.
Within this frame, you are central,
you are sudden, you are unnerving,
you are stamping on the spot as if in tantrum,
you are running circles, you are running a figure eight.
Your hands flap like wet rags in a wind.
Your face is turning itself into throat.

Yards of ocean separate us.
Sea is spilling from my ears.
My mouth is full of mouth-piece.

Then your sound comes
skimming over the water like a flat stone:
it is almost too high to hear.

Stonefish

Pablo got stung
messing about in the shallows
where the seaweed was.

We gathered round
as he gave us his palm:
a small green-ink stain,

tattooed to his life-line.
Pablo's father shouted Spanish
when he saw it,

brought the mother running
with a half-moon of melon
still in her hand.

The car left a trail of dust
                    hanging in the air,
and the day seemed suddenly becalmed.

Rock Fancies Movement

Rock fancies the movement of bird: the flap
of wings, the lift-off, the flight. Rock
fancies taking great strides across pasture,
feeling light among buttercups. Rock
likes to ponder the prospect of stretch
and run, the notions of *fast* and *feather-weight*.

Sometimes,
after a big build-up,
rock manages a moment of budge.
It comes as a shock, bouncing the Richter scale.
Roads rip, rivers rise. The valley thudders in surprise.
Rock wants to join in the celebrations, but grin
has set into gorge. Rock pauses.

Julie Rainsbury

Daughter

She stands
flimsy in white lawn –
laced and tucked
precious
as a christening gown.
Her web of hair
blazes light
across the counterpane.

Daughter –
a blood word
fills my mouth,
empties the room.

Tonight again
she came between us,
high-stepping
on wax toes,
unwound sheets
and slithered
cold into our bed.

I can't reach beyond her.
My outstretched hand
rests on a chill
of feathered breathing.
She is close
and you
are on the other side.

Day at the Sea

Today we went to the end
of the peninsula, jumped
from a high, sea wall
to meet the waves, waded
into the tug and suck of ocean,
just some remembered shift
of shore beneath our feet.

This evening, in the restaurant,
windows hung open above water.
Breeze stirred an edge of curtain,
streamered our candle flame.
Just for you, coloured sails
finned out across the bay.
You turned your half-lit face
to catch their leaving.

Tonight your body is rinsed
of all encumbrance.
I know your clean, white bones,
each pebbled hip, elbow and ankle,
your chest ribbed as sand.
The print of your flesh
lies heavy – here
on my starfish hand.

Hearing Voices

1

All day I hear voices across the water,
a throat's bubble of laughter
that comes to me without a smile.
Sound travels but no one
hoists a flag on nearby islands.

Nights are not quiet either.
Mice skitter in corners
and a hoot or cough can catch
the breath of darkness waiting.

I stack logs
in a blue enamel stove.
Metal burns my fingers,
an undercurrent of flesh to pine.

All the time he talks at me,
rocks forward, back.
His face cuts
across the oil-lamp's beacon,
is segmented into strangers
who haunt our room.

We play word games at the table,
score points,
turn our mock-ivory pieces
into meaning.

2

He balances
on the far peninsula,
lays out barbs on a rock.

I dandle my legs in water,
try to soothe blueberry scratches
that net my ankles.
Small waves hiss, whisper
from crannies
just below the surface.

Fish flick closer,
transparent scraps

of pearl and pewter,
too shining and too small.
He keeps his back turned all morning,
casts and casts,
heaps slivers of hurt
that thrash between us.

Sky bruises black above his shoulder.
The lake licks its lip
and voices chorus in a shout of wind.
Summer hail is loud
and urgent
as I race for shelter.

In a shroud of ice, he still gathers fish.
I look back to see them sliding,
red-scaled, through his hands.

Requiem

'What if this present were the world's last night?'
(John Donne 1571?-1631)

1

We pass Port Talbot on the motorway
at digital no-where hour, the border,
with Mozart on our tape-deck. The car sways
a contra-flow through steel-starred light, water
slick as oil and all the midnight twilight
of summer sky crumbled into cinder
cloud and flame. A moth's sudden, broken flight
obliterated by windscreen wipers.
A soft sibilance sighs beyond the plant,
the unseen sea's long forgotten whisper

that reels us into darkness, backs the chant
of wave on wave of music from the choir –

unanswered pleas – *Kyrie Eleison,*
Christe, Christe, Kyrie Eleison.

2

Fire is too lively for the world's last night:
imagine short days stripped to bone, green fields
salted, all colour gone, just white on white,
streets a knife-sharp glitter and people peeled
by cold. The churchyard walls are fierce with flint,
hold holes of darkness. Snow falls flake on flake:
great rivers still and supple-scaled fish glint –
rigid stains in glass. Trees are exposed, scrape
like chalk against the sky. Birds become stone,
plummet as sap turns brittle in the stem.
Snow falls on snow: swaddles each one alone
in a bivouac of ice. The last steam

of breath freezes to a casket whose sheen
hopes to hold us, slippery, growing green.

3

Another time, a chapel repair fund
draws us to Requiem. A famous choir,
unlit, tiered in an ebb of sunlight, some
resplendent in evening dress. Children tear
around the graveyard, are caught and straightened
by their Mams. It's that almost perfect hour
when all the day's small brightnesses heighten
before subtle dusk. Arched windows are scoured
of shining, shadows break over crisp-haired
wives gaudy in their serious ear-rings.

Music fills the chapel, a loud sea snared
in shell. We're enthralled in this darkening,

astonished that ancient words can lure us
toward the haven of *Benedictus*.

The Prisoner's Tale

Genoa, 1298

Spirit voices lure me
through Kashmiri mountains.
The bones and horns of sheep
are piled in snow
to guide my path.

After forty days, the ocean.
Peregrine falcons nest
and the bird called
bargherlac.
No other living thing.
I've come so far
the Pole Star blinks
where South should be.

Magicians make idols speak,
weave spells to change weather.

The great Khan rides
through walled gardens,
a leopard crouched
on the rump of his horse.
His reed palace
is looped by cords,
its roof clasped
in a dragon's claw.

His barley without husk,
his milk from a white mare,
he steals sun and moon
to blaze his emblem.

In a province called Darkness
the cold is bitter,
faces colourless.
I make fires of green cane
that twist and spit
a whip-crack
to keep animals at bay.
My saddle's hung
with stoat and ermine,
squirrel and black fox.

I travel on a mare
whose foal has been left
on the border of light.

Lynne Rees

Fat

Skinny women order his fish
fried in low-cholesterol oil,
batter as crisp and sheer as glass.

He teases them about goose-fat,
the slip of it, how it dimples
under fingertips, at the right point
of tenderness how it gives
to the tip of a tongue.

He dreams of women
whose flesh parts for him
like lard – their overlap, the spill
and pleat of them, his hands skating
over their suety gleam, their excess
rejoicing under his palms.

Limpets

We all heard the mass ungluing
– a huge suck in reverse – then spitting,
before we rushed to the cove to see them
lolloping on their one broad foot away
from the shore, their little bronchial fringes
shimmering like hula skirts in the night air.

All along the coast this unimagined
exodus from nibbled rocks, the roads sticky
with tracks and the walls of our homes
besieged by urgent raspings. Then
at first light the streets ragged
with gulls, the rattling of cones.

Wings

He struck a deal – a picture
for a pair of wings for the day –
so he drew a rampant horse
or rather a suggestion of a horse
thick calligraphic brush strokes
insinuating a mane, flared nostrils
the silence of rearing hooves.

As each line charged the paper
wing buds grew, pushing through the skin
between his shoulder blades
nudging the shirt on his back.
By the time he put the drawing in the post
flight feathers had ripped the cloth
were fanning the air, ready for take-off.

He was up before he made it home
marvelling at the tarmac on the lane
overviews of fields and trees
places of old promise calling to him –
the plateau at Borobudur, The Ivory Coast
blue green fractals of Madagascar.

He figured he could see them all
if he drew a horse a day, each one quicker
than the last, ink still drying as he rose
but it was never quite the same again –
that first flight, his hands and feet
unable to believe their irrelevance.

Teaching a Chicken to Swim

Each Sunday she unwrapped a pimpled bird
from its cardboard tray and cling film,
cut away the string to free the headless body
– loosening wings and plump, bound hips –
and gently laid it in the bath. Sometimes
the water filled the yawning hole
or leaked between flesh and skin
and bubbled into blisters. She persevered,
couching the bird in open hands,
urging it to try, to slice the water
with its featherless, aerodynamic wings.
She needed the inert frame to pull away,
splaying those irregular fins,
and march its cropped and wanting legs
along the length of bath, turning at each end
as neatly as a chicken on a spit. She needed
just one successful launch.

Dan Rhodes

Russians

I introduced my girlfriend to my friends, but she was so jealous of their pretty Russian wives that the evening was a disaster. She kept announcing that all they ever ate was potatoes, and that Chekhov, Lenin and Solzhenitsyn were so stupid that they could hardly even wipe their own arses.

Surprise

My girlfriend arranged a surprise get-together for all her boyfriends. She said she thought it would be a nice opportunity for us to get to know each other, and that we were sure to find we had all sorts of things in common. After handing around some delicious vol-au-vents, she left us to it. Between sobs we found we'd had absolutely no idea about each other, that we still loved her no matter what, and that we thought the freckles on her little nose were just about the prettiest things in the world.

Funny

My girlfriend told me she was leaving. I was heartbroken, but she was very kind about the whole business. She tried to encourage me to see the funny side of the situation. 'You always said I'd leave you for somebody else,' she said, chuckling and gently patting my arm. 'And now I have.'

Sarah Salway

Leading the Dance

Deborah has ruined his life. It's important that she knows this. Does she know what it feels like for a man to have someone chipping away at his very being? Does she know? Does she? It's no wonder he gets angry with them all. He can't help it. It's not his fault.

He doesn't often hit out, but then he doesn't have to. A look, a word and they get the message. They're well trained. They walk carefully, don't make any noise, don't get in the way. For a child to cry during one of daddy's moods is not a good thing because then he'll teach them how it really feels to hurt.

They all act, but he's the best at it. He's the smiling matchstick man on Father's Day cards, the clown at birthday parties, the cheque-signer on shopping sprees. They're so lucky to have a man like him. So lucky.

(The more Deborah says 'lucky' the odder it becomes. Words are like that. They let you down when you need them most. 'Friend' is another one. See how ugly it is when you really look at it. The letters aren't easy together. It doesn't feel right in the mouth either. It twists the jaw, gets stuck in the back of the throat so you gag. Better to stick to words that get straight to the point. Words like 'strike'. You spit it out before you know what you are doing. You can't help it. It's not your fault.)

It's the fact that she's expecting him to go to a school ceilidh that's the problem. For him. To go to a dance. At the School. Doesn't she realise he's made for better things? Doesn't she feel guilty she's dragged him down to this level? But then she doesn't want to go to the dance either. Not with him. He'll be the life and soul, everyone will want to dance with him, he'll whirl the children round too fast, get them too excited and then they'll all go home together. Alone.

156

She can't even dance. She'll try to lead the way she always does. This is another of her problems. She's incapable of letting herself go with him. If only she would. If only she would do things the way he says then everything would be alright. Why does she always have to fight? Why can't she try to follow him just once? Will she try? Will she? He supposes he might make the effort to go to the dance. For the children's sake. For Deborah's sake. For the sake of the family. It's only a bloody dance. He used to love to dance.

★

It's at times like this she wishes she had a knife. She can feel its weight in her hand, the ridges in the metal as her fingers cup round the handle. It has to be sharp. Running it along her arm so the point makes ripples in the hairs, she'll finally understand what it means to be on knife-edge.

It's her nerve ends she wants to cut away, the ones on her fingertips, on her tongue, between her legs. She can feel them now. Even now, she's melting. He can always do this to her. He's right. She is pathetic, but oh god the way he kisses. What that man can do with his lips, his tongue, his fingers. No one kisses like him.

★

Deborah's watching him now as he dances round her, deliberately twisting his hips as he passes so the fabric from his kilt brushes against her. A woman at the table starts to clap her hands in time to the music, but Deborah knows it's his feet she's applauding. Clap, clap, clap. Clap, clap, clap. It's a man's dance, a dance for men in skirts. They're all wearing the kilt tonight. They're all bravehearts with a passion. It took an Australian and an Irish film star to show them how good they could look, but they've learnt the lesson well. T-shirts and tartan are the new order of the day, and he's looking the best. And he knows it.

He's standing in front of her, holding out his hand. She's careful not to take it. She accepts it instead. Oh yes, he's taught her the difference. She's passive as she lets her hand lie in his and he rewards her with a bow and then a smile. They walk to the dance floor and stand opposite each other, eyes locked. His mouth is counting – *one, two, three, four* – and then he bows again and she curtseys. The dance begins.

They're cautious to begin with, but then there are others laughing and she catches his eye. He nods his head. It's going to be alright. The music's taking over. They become nothing more than the cogs that feed the machine as she receives first one man and then another, bending down now to twirl a small boy, passing him on to the next in line and then it's their turn. She winces as he twists her wrists too tightly and she's spinning, too fast, too fast, but just in time he stops her, hands her over with a click. She takes each outstretched arm that clamours for hers, refusing none, turning round and round and back to him. Always back to him.

He becomes her safety net as she pounds against him again and again and again. *One, two, three, four...* The line stretches on for ever and then it's his turn. They're back at the beginning. The clapping echoes in her head and she becomes whatever he wants her to be. She's lost herself as her feet start to stamp, her hands pull together and her head bobs up and down. She aches from smiling.

Eventually the music has to stop and she clutches at him to keep upright. He holds her tight, pulling her head back on to his chest as they walk so she feels like a ventriloquist dummy, treading on his toes. She stands up straight, away from him, hearing the hiss too late. When she turns to take his hand, he won't give it to her the way she gave him hers.

At the table, she's so keen to get back to how they were that she lets him yank her down by the hair on to his knee. He plays with her fingers, beating out the music on her shoulders, joggling her up and down. Deborah sits there, unable to join in adult conversations because he's turned her into a child. This is how he likes her. This is how he's happy.

He's calling her name softly now – Deb...or...rah, Deb...or...rah – whispering so she has to lean back to rest her ear against his mouth. 'How could you, Deborah?' It's not the words but his breath blowing over her skin she hears.

'Don't you know what you've done to me?' She looks at him as he continues beaming round the table, his thick arms crossed over in front of her stomach and she squeezes that thin sliver of steel in her clenched fist.

Everyone's quiet as they watch a blue-faced warrior sitting cross-legged on stage tapping out a lament on African drums. Only the children are still twirling on the dance floor, eyes shut as they bump into each other but then they get too wild. Some start to cry. It's time to take them home anyway, put them to bed, share a whisky and a quiet chat together. It's been a good evening.

They follow the crowd out of the school hall. He is carrying a child with one arm, the other tight around her wrist. She watches the families go and knows there are many who envy her having a man who touches her so often, holds her so close.

When, finally, it's their turn to go through the door he rubs his face into her hair and she can hear him humming. She listens frantically, trying to make sense of the noises he's making but, too soon, he pushes her out in the evening air and she has to shut her eyes tight against the icy wind that slaps at her face. She will never understand him. He'll tell her later. When they're home. When they're alone.

In Good Order

I'm trying to be a writer so it is very important I keep my bookshelves in good order.

It has taken me a long time to find the best system, but now I arrange my books alphabetically, using the first letter of the author's surname. This would work well if my wife didn't keep picking books out to read and then putting them back at random. Elaine doesn't seem to realise that the irritation of finding a C in the P shelf can put me off writing for the rest of the day.

'It's easy,' I tell her as I explain the system once more, sounding the letters out phonetically as you would to a child.

'They're all just stories at the end of the day,' she says. 'Why does it matter?'

'It's my Work,' I say. I wish I didn't have to keep reminding her that writing isn't about having fun. She will insist on calling it my hobby.

'Oh, your work.' To make a joke of it, she thrusts her chin in and out like a turkey gobbling. The skin on her neck creases and puckers as she moves. I don't think she would do this if she knew how unattractive it made her look.

'Tell me a story, David,' she says and then she sighs. 'Don't you remember how you used tell me such lovely stories? I thought you were the cleverest man in the world.'

I ignore this. I'm determined to prove my point. 'I'll tell you what,' I say. 'Give me the name of any book and I'll find it straight away.'

'Birdsong,' she says. I turn to the F's and pull it out immediately, handing it to her in triumph.

Elaine looks at the cover. 'Shouldn't that be in the P's for Phoulks,' she says, aping my earlier pronunciation. She pouts her lips forward with the 'ph' sound as if she's asking for a kiss but I ignore her and turn back to my writing. I feel I've proved my point but when I look round, I notice she's gone and so has the book.

I try to forget about it but I can't. I go over to the shelves but it's not in the F's. I try the P's because Elaine always takes jokes too far but there's no sign there either. I skim the S's for Sebastian and then the B's. Eventually, I'm forced to go and find her.

She's in the kitchen, cutting up a lump of meat into cubes for a casserole. She makes me wait until she's finished putting each chunk into the sizzling oil, turning them over and over to brown on all sides. She wipes her hands quickly on her apron.

'Where have you looked?' It's as if she thinks we're playing a game. I go through the letters until she stops me.

'Why B?' she asks.

'For book, of course.' I'm so cross I reply without thinking, but then I realise how ridiculous this sounds. Knowing this, I'm even more furious when she laughs so loudly. It's not that funny.

'Guess where I've put it?' She holds out her hands as if to show me she's not got it on her. A tiny globule of meat is still stuck to her middle finger, a red smear I think must be blood on the nail.

'I don't want to guess.' It's hard to be patient. 'I just want it back.'

'Well, it's next to *The Rachel Papers*,' she laughs.

'Martin Amis!' I look at her for a minute trying to work out the connection, but then I give up.

She looks like a cat who has got the cream and reluctantly, still thinking of the raw meat she's just been touching, I take her outstretched hand as she pulls me back to the sitting room.

'They are the same colour.' She points to the two red book covers. 'Think of the difference this will make to our reading. Feeling black?' She pulls out a book with a black spine. 'Here's *The Bell Jar*. Hey, it works.' Elaine starts to take books out with both hands and I see she has formed a rainbow with them. 'Our shelves will be so pretty we need never buy another painting,' she says.

'Why do you always have to mock me?' I ask. 'Why can't you just let me have my own system?'

'Let me tell you a story, David,' she says. I shake my head but her eyes seem to be locked into mine. I can't look away. Her voice takes on a singsong quality that makes acid rise in my stomach. This, and the way her bloodstained fingers are fluttering by her sides, makes me want to be sick. I cover my mouth with my hand as I listen to her.

'There was once a man who loved words,' she says, 'and in return, they danced and sang and moved for him in a way that made everyone who heard them feel joyful. But then one day, he met a big, bad system who whispered into his ear that just playing with words was not enough. Having fun was all very well and while words were fine as far as they went, what the

161

man really needed was a system to look after him. Now, I don't know if you've met any systems but they like to eat dreams best of all and the one this man found was a particularly hungry system...'

Somehow I find the strength to leave the room. I go upstairs to wash my face and hands and when I come back, Elaine's gone so I spend a few minutes putting away all the books she's left just lying around. Then I notice something. I go to find the ruler and stand in front of the bookshelves pulling the inch rod out and letting it spring back a few times. I write the alphabet down on a piece of paper and make a grid before setting to work measuring each section:

A	2 feet 3 inches
B	4 feet 2 inches

I have just reached V when Elaine comes back into the room.

'What are you doing now?' she asks, and picks up my graph. 'Are you going to make them all the same length? Buy only authors who have surnames beginning with E or J to make it fair. You could start a campaign. Equal rights for the initial I!' She squints down the page. 'Hey, there's only an inch of I's. That's discrimination.'

It's hard to imagine that there was a time when my wife and I were happy. Indeed, we used to agree on almost everything and it's the memory of this that forces me to at least try to explain what I've found. I want so much to be able to make her understand.

'It must be the way people buy books,' I say. 'You and I are pretty catholic in our reading tastes but you can see how many B's we have. What if people buy books because of where they are displayed on the shelves in the book shop rather than how interesting they are?'

'But our initial is ffff for Ford,' she says.

'Exactly.' I check the graph carefully. 'We've only 11 inches of F's so that's not a very good omen, is it?'

She nods, running her finger along the letters. 'You could always change your initial to B,' she says, and I think I've finally got through to her. But then before she leaves the room, she stops and stands in the doorway for a moment and I know she's waiting for me to try it out.

'David Bored,' I whisper and I can hear her cackling as she goes down the stairs.

An hour later, at seven o'clock, I'm hungry so I go down to the kitchen to see if the casserole is ready. Instead of the supper I'm anticipating, Elaine is lying naked on the kitchen table, her arms and legs stretched out as wide as she can make them. Her body is covered in books.

'It's your choice,' she whispers. 'The system or me.'

I am sure Elaine never used to be so dramatic. I stand, resting my hands against the edge of the table and look down at her for a few minutes. Her head is twisted to one side, pinned down by the weight of a Vikram Seth.

Slowly, systematically, I remove the books from my wife's body. An Atwood covers her right breast, Brecht her left. I find Carver at her elbow, Dickens in the hollow on her chestbone. Eliot balances on one knee. Forster sinks out of sight into her navel while Mrs Gaskell sits upright against her neck. Hardy cups her belly and Isherwood rests on her chin. I work my way through them until finally, as I take the Zolas from her feet, Elaine leaps up and runs out the door.

My arms are too full of books to stop her but I don't move anyway. I've had all the stories I can take for one day.

Victor Tapner

Thames Idol

A scarred hand carved my buttocks
scraped my spine
made thin hips to cup a man

I stood at the back of a quiet hut
In famine they brought me food
in spring they sang for rain

At last they gave me to the river
a bigger god than I
Earth pressed my breasts

Now I cheat the rot of leaves
Black water fills my eyes
frost cracks my grained flesh

Your hand will draw me from the mud
Find me in your own time
find me in your own face

Grime's Graves

Axes of antler
ox-bone scoops
spring and summer
on our bellies
down here stripping flint

the sky passes

Chalk-torn faces
splinters chip our eyes

breath sore
dragging bags
of rock and rubble

our raw tomb opens

Picks clack
a half-blind curse
a cough a clot of grit
walls seep
a roof crack loosens

the tunnel listens

Sun high the ladder
sheep-curd milk and bread
spring and summer
fields of fresh light

below a crawl
to the day's last stone

Coffee Shop

Most evenings
he comes in
about this time.

Espresso,
cigarette,
an intelligent paper.

A seat
by the window,
facing in.

Jeans, jumper
and black brogues.
I like those.

I wipe the table,
sometimes twice.
When I lean over

with his cup
my apron tightens,
just a touch.

Most evenings
he comes in
about this time.

I always think
he won't.
And then he does.

Gaudí Declares His Love For Pepita

It is evening
in the soft Mataró sun
her room is quiet
her clock
ticks away his words

He stands
outside the door
no flowers in his hands
just sweat on his palms
and on his clothes
the soft dust of masonry
from the yard

And then she says come in
and he goes in
and hesitates
and tries to ask

And so she smiles to hide a laugh
and says she can't
and didn't he know
and didn't he know

And after that
alone
he toils on:
God's architect on earth
the great towers
towering in his mind

soft needles
rising
in the Barcelona night
the soft dust
of masonry on his clothes

Caryl Ward

Everybody Tells Fibs Sometimes

Mrs Richards is calling my name, and I can't move. I feel all stiff, and I feel sick and hot and cold at the same time, like when I was in bed with flu. She's calling my name again, louder, and she's looking straight at me, and her eyes are like the small coal that burns a lot longer than the big lumps.

I close my exercise-book, although I know I'll have to open it again in a minute, and I wish it wasn't my name that's on the cover. They keep their heads down when I go past the desks, and it's only Terry Rees, who's got black curly hair and lips so red that he looks like he's got lipstick on, that turns his head round and watches me. Terry Rees is Mrs Richards's favourite. He's got eyes and eyelashes like Jem, our Jersey cow, and he doesn't wear grey shorts and navy or bottle-green jumpers like the other boys. He wears long fawn trousers like as if he's grown-up, and all his jumpers are either pale blue, or yellow, or red to match his lips. And he's got a different sort of coat to everyone else, with a zip instead of buttons, and it doesn't come down over his bum, so he must get colds on his kidneys. And his mother and sister are different too. They live down The Green, next door to the Gwilyms, and all the council houses are the same outside, and they're all the same inside, and they've all got the same sort of furniture, at least the ones that don't have net curtains do, and Terry Rees's house doesn't have net curtains, so it's funny really that he's different.

I put my book on Mrs Richards' desk and open it to the page, and there's all the numbers in the little red squares, and the times and divide signs and the two lines at the bottom with the answers in between, and they're wrong – I know they're wrong. I step back and look at my shoes, but I can see Terry Rees watching, and I can see Mrs Richards slashing the page with big red crosses. And she's telling me I've got nought out of ten, nought out of ten, and she's saying it louder and louder, and Christine Thomas and Pam Marshall, who sit together in the front desk middle row and are always top of the class – both of them, are nudging each other and smiling like cats that have just been fed because they got ten out of ten. And Mrs Richards is telling me to say the nine times table out loud, and although I know it, I can't say it, and she's on her feet and her sharp knuckles are poking me in the chest and she's telling me I'm dull, dull, dull, and I'll never pass the scholarship. And everybody's looking now, and she's jigging round me and her fists are jabbing like a boxer's except that there's nobody to fight. I think Mrs Richards would like a fight. Like the one between Morgan Mounty's father and Mr Davies.

Mr Davies had given Morgan Mounty two cracks that morning. And Morgan Mounty told his father when he went home for dinner, and his father and Morgan Mounty marched into the playground and asked for Mr Davies. And Miss James, who was on playground duty went to fetch Mr Davies, and Morgan Mounty's father hit him straight in the face. And Mr Davies looked as if he didn't know what had hit him, and Morgan Mounty's father kept saying, 'Come on you bastard, have a go at me.' And Mr Davies said he didn't want to fight, but he had to a bit, because Morgan Mounty's father kept on punching, and Mr Davies was just like the loser, the one up against the ropes with his hands up. And everybody was in a ring around them, and some people were cheering, and then Mr Griffiths came out and threatened to call the police, and Morgan Mounty's father went off down the road swinging his hairy arms and walking like a gorilla. Then the bell went, and we were all lining up to go in, and Morgan Mounty said he was sorry he'd said about the cracks because they'd come straight back to the school, and he hadn't had his dinner, and he was starving, and the cracks didn't hurt much anyway. And everybody was saying that it's best not to tell your mother or your father if you get a crack, because they're bound to say you've done wrong. And Roy Watts said that when he was in Standard One, he had six cracks off Mr Richards in Mr

Richards's room, and nobody saw, and Roy didn't tell, but somehow or other Roy Watts's father heard about the cracks two days later and gave Roy Watts the belt, and it hurt a lot more than the cracks did. That was the time that Roy Watts took his thing out in the boys' playground and peed over the back of Mary Denver's dress through the railings, and it was new that week, red and white gingham with plenty of gathers. So it just goes to show what can happen if you tell.

And Mrs Richards is punching with her knuckles, and my chest is hurting, and I wish she'd go away for a nervous breakdown, which is a sort of holiday, like she did when we had the supply teacher instead. And she's telling me that I've got to stay in at playtime and do them over, and I'm dull and I won't pass the scholarship.

Everybody wants to pass the scholarship because you go on the bus every day and you wear a navy-blue uniform and a tie and a hat with a red band and a badge with the school thingy on it in Latin so that nobody knows what it means. And you have a leather satchel for your books that pulls your shoulder down. And everybody looks the same and very smart. If you don't pass you go the other side of the wall, to the seniors, and you just wear the same sort of things you always wear. And when you leave you go to work down the arsenal that some people are starting to call the trading estate, and you leave your curlers in all day and wear a headscarf and be common or cheap.

But I'm not going to the arsenal. If I don't pass, I'm going to the Convent. You don't have to be Catholic, and you don't have to pass anything. It's a good school, and anyone can go so long as you pay. But Daddy says he could do without the expense, and we've got to get a new tractor because ours is always conking out lately. And the uniform is brown, not nigger brown, shitty brown.

When Mummy has her light coats dyed, she always has either navy blue or nigger brown because they're serviceable. I know that navy blue is the blue that the sailors in the navy wear. But when we were getting Mummy's coat out of the cleaners one day, she couldn't find the ticket, and the lady asked what colour it was, and Mummy said brown, and the lady still couldn't find it, and she asked what colour brown, and Mummy said nigger brown, and the lady found it straight away. And I asked why did they call it nigger brown, and what's nigger. And Mummy and the lady didn't answer, and Mummy looked at me the way she does when she tells me I should be ashamed of myself, so I never asked again.

There's only one girl from the village who goes to the Convent. She's almost grown-up, and she never looks at anybody. If I went there, I'd have to change buses, and I've never changed on my own, and I might get on the wrong bus. And although it's a seaside place, it's nowhere near the front – so it might as well be anywhere. I've been past it on the bus, and I don't like it. There's a big high wall all around it, so you can't see it. All the teachers are nuns, and they're all ladies. I like men teachers best. I've seen some of the nuns, four of them. They were walking down the path that leads to Newton beach, one behind the other, like penguins. And they weren't talking – but they don't, they pray all the time, on their knees.

I tried it a few times on my knees. It was just before last Christmas when I was asking God to make sure that Father Christmas brought me a two-wheeler. And he did, a red one, with a basket on the front, exactly the right size. I tried to keep it up after Christmas, but the mat on the floor by my bed kept slipping and when I used to get up my knees were red. So now I pray in bed, on my back, looking up at the ceiling, which makes more sense because that's where He is – up there.

It's four years before we've got to pass. Well, three before the first try, but that doesn't matter because hardly anybody passes first try, and you just try again. The teachers started talking about it after we came back after the summer holidays, and every day they say something about it. So I thought I'd make an early start, and every night when I've finished the 'God Blesses' I ask Him to *please* make me pass, so by the time it comes round He will have plenty of time. And it's not only Arithmetic and Mental in the scholarship, it's composition, and I'm good at that, and I'm the best reader in the class. It's true – I'm not telling lies – Mr Pugh told me.

*

Pat Griffiths is reading, and we're all following in our Beacon Readers Number 3 – that's the yellow one. There's never enough Beacon Readers, and I'm sharing with my friend Anne. Pat Griffiths keeps stopping, so it's taking a long time. Mr Pugh never asks the good readers to read.

The aniseed gobstopper that I bought in Tizzy's feels rough on my tongue, the way it feels when it's about half-way to the seed in the middle. I take it out to have a look what colour it is, and it's just at that sort of pinkish bluish stage, before it turns to grey. It might last till home time before it gets to the seed.

Beacon Reader Number 3 is boring, there's no good stories in it. And Number 4 – that's the orange one – is just as bad. I read it the week that I had a bad chest, and had to stay in at playtimes because my mother sent a note. You're not supposed to read the Beacon Readers except in Reading. They keep them in the cupboard, with the chalk and dusters, and the black daps that aren't pairs. They've got 'Glamorgan Education Authority' stamped inside the covers, and some of them are stamped over the writing too, and you're not allowed to take them home – nobody is.

Mr Pugh is telling Pat Griffiths to stop, and everybody's wondering who will be next. It won't be David Finch or Mary Denver because they read yesterday. Leila Watkins is crouching down in her seat, like a dog. He hasn't made her so far this week. Leila Watkins stutters, she always has.

But Mr Pugh is asking us, 'What is the meaning of Christmas?' That's because it's in three weeks, and the Beacon Readers story is about a family sitting around a Christmas tree opening their presents. And the father had a tie, and the mother had a brooch – Pat Griffiths didn't know brooch – and the girl got a tea-set for her doll – which I thought was very childish – and the boy got a fountain pen, and writing paper and envelopes – Pat didn't get envelopes either – and a stamp collection. And they were all very pleased with what they got. Then they all had dinner, and it was about

172

what they were eating which was turkey and Christmas pudding, and the girl found the silver sixpence. And Mr Pugh is saying that Christmas isn't just presents and eating, and that it's Jesus's birthday, and then he's asking, 'Hands up who has turkey for dinner on Christmas Day?' and lots of people put their hands up. Then he says, 'Hands up who has chicken?' and the chickens are in the lead. I wait for him to say hands up for goose, but he doesn't, and he doesn't ask for duck either, and Aunty Peggy and Elizabeth always have one, and she says there's plenty of meat on a duck for two.

Mr Pugh is asking what presents people hope to get for Christmas, and almost everybody who hasn't got a bike wants one. Two of the boys want three-speed drop-handled racers, but they think they'll have to wait until they pass the scholarship. Penny Fields wants a pony, but she thinks she'll have to wait till her twenty-first birthday because her brother had to wait till he was twenty-one to get his MG. Vera King and Diane Preddy both want watches, and Gwyn Evans wants his own radio, and Mervyn Williams wants a television because the one his Dad got had to go back. I want lots of books, with real stories in them like they've got in the library. There isn't a library in the village, so we can only go in the school holidays, and then you can only have two out at a time, but when I grow up I'm going to have a room in my house with books up to the ceiling like the library. And Mummy's having electric for Christmas. Well, she won't actually get it until the spring, because it's got to come out from the village, and that takes time. And it's going to cost an awful lot, because Idwal on the next farm to us was going to have it as well, but now Idwal says he's not having it, and Daddy's got to pay the whole lot himself. And Daddy says they're charging enough to bankrupt a man. And Ifor Tal-y-Garn was bankrupted, and I heard him tell daddy, 'They took the bloody lot.' He didn't say who the robbers were, and there's new people living in Tal-y-Garn now, and Ifor Tal-y-Garn is living with his sister and working in the foundry, and he's on the bottle.

Gwyn Evans is asking Mr Pugh is there *really* a Father Christmas, and some people are shouting that there isn't. And

Mr Pugh says, 'Hands up who believes in Father Christmas', and lots of people put their hands up straight away, and Morgan Mounty and Roy Watts are shouting that there's not, and some people are putting them up, and taking them down, and putting them up again. So Mr Pugh says, 'All right, hands up who doesn't believe in Father Christmas.' And Morgan Mounty's gang have got their hands up, and lots of people are up and down with their hands. And Morgan Mounty is saying that it's his Dad, that it's everybody's Dad, and Terry Rees says it can't be because he hasn't got a Dad, so Morgan Mounty says it's his Mum then, and the believers and the non-believers are shouting at each other, and Mr Pugh bangs on his desk and shouts 'Order. Quiet'. And he keeps banging the desk and we go quiet, and he says, 'Hands on Heads'.

Then Terry Rees takes his hand off his head, and puts it up and he's saying, 'But is there a Father Christmas, Sir? Tell us Sir,' and Mr Pugh says 'No.'

And he starts going on about Santa Claus and traditions, and I look sideways at Anne, and she looks like she's trying not to cry. And I try not to listen to what he's saying, and pull my arms tight into the side of my head like a bird folding its wings, and I try to make my elbows touch in front of my face. And although I'm not listening to Mr Pugh, he must be right, teachers don't tell lies, and although I tell fibs sometimes, everybody tells fibs sometimes, he must be right, he *must* be right.

At last, Mr Pugh is shaking the brass bell with the wooden handle, and the message is clanging out loud and clear, 'There's no Father Christmas, there's no Father Christmas, there's no...' and I'm pushing through the mob, to my peg in the cloakroom, and running out through the door, and the gate, running past the Senior School, where I catch the bus to go home. On around the corner, where the mothers are coming out of the clinic, pushing their babies in prams and saying, 'He's gained two pounds this week, they told me to put him on solids.' 'There's no Father Christmas, there's no Father Christmas.'

Past Tizzy's shop, which isn't really a shop, just a wooden shed with a tin roof, where Tizzy, who everybody says is over a hundred, sells sweets and apples that are rotten in the middle and bananas that are going black, but everybody goes there, although it's further from the school than Lewis's, which is only across the road, because you can have one of anything from Tizzy's.

Across the railway bridge, with the train that's going to Cardiff, and then Paddington, London, puffing along underneath. 'There's no Father Christmas, there's no Father Christmas, there's no Father...'

Down the hill, past the Post Office, and past Evans's where my mother puts things on the book, with its high, polished mahogany counters, and the big glass jars of sweets lined up on the top shelf by the ceiling, where Megan has to climb up the ladder to get them down. And sometimes when I can't make up my mind whether I want to suck the sherbet out of the little holes in the ends of sherbet lemons, or bite the red and yellow coconut from the liquorice allsorts and keep the black bits till last, or just to have two ounces of boiled mixture, which is sensible because they last longest, she goes up the ladder two or three times and weighs me out a special two-ounce mix. 'There's no Father Christmas, there's no Father Christmas, there's no...'

Past the monument, with the names of the soldiers that died in the war, and the angel with the big wings on top, that Gerald, our workman, says is the only virgin in the village, and round the corner past the Rec, with the roundabout that's been broken for over six months now, and the black-painted Nursery School that looks like a caravan without wheels, that I was on the waiting list for, and that I went to for one day. But when I went, they found they were a cot short after dinner and they didn't know where to put me, and I told them that I never went to bed after dinner anyway, and Mummy was always telling people that if I went to sleep after dinner I wouldn't go to sleep when I went to bed, but they wouldn't take any notice of me, and when Mummy came to fetch me home, they told her that they were full-up and didn't have room for me, but that I'd be first on the waiting list again. 'There's no Father Christmas, there's no Father Christmas, there's no...'

Over the bridge across the river, with the stone sides that I walk along with Anne and Jenny, with my arms out trying not to look down at the water. I know it's deep because we dipped the sheep in it a bit further down before shearing last year, and Jack Wag's wife drowned in it years ago because she thought she had cancer, and Daddy found her body. 'There's no Father Christmas, there's no Father Christmas, there's no...'

I have to stop to push open the kissing-gate, with its black paint and big spots of rust; its hinges groan like a cow dying, and I drop my coat. The kissing-gate is for lovers to stand and kiss in. But they never kiss there, they kiss sitting on the grass further over the Gweunydd, down by the bend in the river, in the little patch behind the blackberry bushes, that you can't see, where the foxgloves always grow. I've seen them kissing in Cae Ffordd too, it was just before Daddy cut the hay there, and the boy was lying on top of the girl, and his trousers were falling down his bum. 'There's no Father Christmas, there's no Father Christmas, there's no...'

The cows in the Gweunydd are under the three big oak trees, where they always go to get out of the rain. Daddy or Uncle Dave will be coming to fetch them for milking before long, and I hope Rosie hasn't got mastitis. I'm halfway over the fence across the gap in the hedge to Cae Ffordd, that's there to stop the sheep getting into the Gweunydd where they might get out onto the road, and my coat is caught on the hedge and I hear the threads pull when I jump off into Cae Ffordd, dragging it after me.

And I'm running across the footpath in Cae Ffordd, where I used to find the little balls and wonder who'd lost them. But that was ages and ages ago, before I knew what the big pinchers that hang on the nail in the corner of the calf-shed are for. And Daddy told me the pinchers don't hurt, but I think the pinchers must hurt, and Daddy told me a fib, but it was only a little fib, and 'There's no Father Christmas, there's no Father Christmas...'

I scrape the backs of my legs getting over the stone stile, and I splash through the muck in the lane, and I go over on my ankle in one of the pot-holes, and it hurts but I can't stop.

And here's Uncle Dave, coming to fetch the cows, and he's got an old sack over his shoulders instead of his oilskin, so he must be soaked through and perishing, and he might catch pneumonia and die. And he's saying, 'Woow! Woow!' like I say to Ginger when I pull the reins tight. And his arms are around me, and I can smell the cattle-cake that's been in the sack, and the wet packet of cigarettes, in his coat, that's got the sailor man with the black beard on the front, and the little cards with the Grand National and Derby winners inside, that me and him save in the empty Milk Tray box that we keep in the right-hand side cupboard in the sideboard. And he's saying,

'Now tell me. Tell me what it's all about.' And I can't tell anyone.

But he's saying, 'Come on, you know you can tell me, and I won't tell anyone.'

So I tell him quick, in one big mouthful, 'Uncle Dave, there's no Father Christmas.' And he doesn't believe me, and he's saying, 'Course there is, course there is.'

And I tell him, 'No there's not. Teacher told us. Teacher told us.'

It's a big shock to Uncle Dave too, because Daddy told us a lie, and Uncle Dave won't be able to say his prayers again either, and he won't be able to be proud of me so he'll have to be ashamed instead. And his eyes are all shiny, and there's big drops of rain running down his face, like the ones I watch on the window, when I pretend that they're having a race to the bottom, and I bet which one will win.

'Teachers aren't always right, cariad. They're not *always* right.' And Uncle Dave is trying to smile at me, and I know he won't tell anyone. He'll never ever tell. He'll just wait for the results to come out – like me.

Acknowledgements

Amanda Dalton
'How to Disappear', 'Out of the Blue', 'The Gifts', 'Nest' are from *How to Disappear* (Bloodaxe, 1999).

Frank Dullaghan
'Crossing' is from *First Pressings* (Faber, 1998). 'Ordnance Survey 24 – West Cork' is from HU, No. 108, Winter 1999. 'Escalator' was accepted by *London Magazine* in October 1999. 'Frames' is from *The Devil,* Issue L, 1999.

Paul Lenehan
'Great Bus Journeys of Dublin' is to be published in *Irish Short Stories 2000* (Phoenix, 2000), edited by David Marcus.

Malcolm Lewis
'The Dream of David Lloyd George' is from *Poetry Wales,* Vol. 34, No. 4, April 1999.

Fiona Owen
'Picnic on Ajman Beach' is from *New Welsh Review,* No. 48, Spring 2000. 'Mother (who can't swim)' is from *Iron,* Issue No. 80, November 1996-February 1997. 'Rock Fancies Movement' is from *New Welsh Review,* No. 42, Autumn 1998.

Julie Rainsbury
'Daughter', 'Day at the Sea', 'Hearing Voices', 'Requiem', 'The Prisoner's Tale' are from *Night Lines* (Gomer, 2000).

Lynne Rees
'Teaching a Chicken to Swim' is from *Iron,* Issue No. 80, November 1996 - February 1997.

Sarah Salway
'Leading the Dance' is from *Buzzwords,* Issue No. 6, June 2000. 'In Good Order is from *GroundSwell,* No. 4, July 2000.

Victor Tapner
'Thames Idol' is from *Lost London – 2000 Years of London,* anthology of prizewinners in the Millennial Poetry Competition, organised by Blue Nose Poets and supported by the Poetry Society and the Museum of London (Blue Nose

Press, 1999). 'Coffee Shop' is from *Can I Sing a Short Song?* the 1998 Dulwich Festival International Poetry Competition anthology (Words & Music at the Dog, 1998).

Biographical Notes

Barbara Bentley started writing seriously in 1991, two years before she undertook an MA in Writing at the University of Glamorgan (1993-1995). She has had some success in major competitions: in 1994, she won first prize in the Charterhouse International Poetry Competition and the Wales Writers' Group Prize in the Cardiff International Poetry Competition. Her first collection of poetry, *Living Next to Leda*, was published in 1996 (Seren). She works at Wigan and Leigh College, where she teaches Literature, Linguistics and Creative Writing to degree level; she is also Head of English and Performing Arts.

Edward Boyne is based in Galway, Ireland. He has had various short stories broadcast on radio and published in journals or anthologies. He is currently completing his first novel which is set in Dublin and London. He is also completing a PhD at Liverpool John Moores University.

Robert Doyle is 28 years old and comes from the seaside village of Ainsdale in the North West of England. He graduated in Humanities and completed the MA in Writing at the University of Glamorgan. During his time as a journalist he has worked for the *Western Mail, Liverpool Echo*, and *Catholic Times*. He is currently freelancing and writing a novel about sexual perversion.

Amanda Dalton was born in Coventry in 1957. She has worked as a Deputy Headteacher, a Centre Director for the Arvon Foundation at Lumb Bank, and is currently Education Director at the Royal Exchange Theatre in Manchester. Her first poetry collection, *How To Disappear* (Bloodaxe Books), was shortlisted for the 1999 Forward Prize for Best First Collection. Her radio play, *Room Of Leaves*, was the BBC Prix Italia entry for 1999. A second radio play will be broadcast on BBC Radio 4 later this year.

Frank Dullaghan was born in Dundalk, Ireland, in 1955. He lives in Essex with his wife and two teenage sons. A man of many talents: an expert in martial arts (judo and karate); a Chief Operating Officer with an on-line investment bank in London; and, last but not least, co-editor of the poetry quarterly *Seam*. His poetry has been published widely in magazines, including: *New Welsh Review, Poetry Wales, The Iron Book of British Haiku, Quadrant, The Rialto, Stand, Verse*. His work was also highly commended in the recent Blue Nose International Poetry Competition.

Richard John Evans is 29, was born in the Rhondda. He has a BA in English and an MA in Creative Writing from the University of Glamorgan, and is currently a journalist with *Wales on Sunday*. His first novel, *Entertainment*, is published by Seren (2000).

Euron Griffith's stories have appeared in various publications including *The New Welsh Review, Iron,* and *The Anglo-Welsh Review*. In 1997 he received a New Writer's Bursary from the Arts Council of Wales and in 1998 his story 'The Beatles in Tonypandy' was included in the US anthology *In My Life* (Fromm, New York). He studied English at the University of Kent and now lives in Cardiff where he works as a broadcaster. He still hasn't finished his novel.

Pamela Johnson has published two novels, *Under Construction* and *Deep Blue Silence*, both with Sceptre. Her poems appear in the anthologies *Riding Pillion* and *Things We Said Today* and she is co-author of a collection of children's stories, *City Summer*. Her critical writing on visual art includes the monograph Michael Brennand-Wood: *You Are Here,* and the collection of essays *Ideas in the Making: Practice in Theory*. She is currently completing a collection of short stories for adults and working on her third novel.

Paul Lenehan, a Dubliner, has had stories published in Ireland, England, Germany, Australia, and now, at last, in Wales. Both of the stories published here came through the creative writing workshops at Glamorgan – many thanks, therefore, are due to his cohort and his tutors. Paul is Assistant Editor of the *Poetry Ireland Review*.

Malcolm Lewis, who is from Caerffili, works in London as a freelance writer. He has had stories and poetry published in

Planet, Poetry London, Poetry Wales and *The Works*. Currently, he writes a music column for *Planet*.

Mo McAuley. Born in Accrington in 1953, now living in Speldhurst, a village in Kent. Her short story 'Looking for Maddie' won the Good Housekeeping / Waterstones short story prize in 1998. She has recently finished a collection of short stories with a working title of *A Death in the Family*, and is currently working on a novel, provisionally called *The Complete Angler*.

Maria McCann was born in Liverpool but has lived in various parts of Britain as well as in France and Greece. For the past thirteen years she has been employed as an FE lecturer in the West Country. Her first novel, *As Meat Loves Salt*, will be published by Flamingo in February 2001.

Fiona Owen. After living abroad for much of her childhood, Fiona Owen has put down roots in Anglesey, where she has lived since 1978. Her work has been published in various magazines and journals - *Scintilla, New Welsh Review, Poetry Wales, Stand, Iron, Staple, Resurgence, The Haiku Quarterly* and others; and is included in the anthologies *Needs Be* ed. David Hart (Flarestack, 1998), *Anglesey Anthology* ed. Dewi Roberts (Gwasg Carreg Gwalch, 1999), *Mama's Baby (Papa's Maybe)* eds. Lewis Davies & Arthur Smith (Parthian, 1999) and *Catwomen from Hell* ed. Janet Thomas (Honno, 2000). She teaches for the Open University and runs courses in creative writing and contemporary Buddhist poetry.

Julie Rainsbury was born and brought up in Kent. After studying for a degree in English Literature at the University of Newcastle upon Tyne, she taught in south-east London and Kent for several years. Married with three grown-up sons, she has lived and worked in West Wales since 1978. In 1993, she won the Welsh Writers' Prize in the Cardiff Poetry Competition and was also awarded a Welsh Arts Council Writer's Bursary. Several of her short stories – both for children and adults – have been broadcast on BBC Radio Wales and have appeared in anthologies. Her main publications are: for children – *The Seventh Seal* (Pont, 1993), *Spellmakers* (Pont, 1999), *Crab-Boy Cranc* (Pont, 2000); shortlisted for the

NASEN children's book award. 2000; her first poetry collection, *Night Lines* was published by Gomer (2000).

Lynne Rees was born and brought up in South Wales. After working for seven years in the Channel Islands she moved to Kent in 1985 where she ran her own second-hand and antiquarian bookshop for eleven years. Since receiving her M.A. in 1996, she has been awarded a Writers' Bursary from South East Arts, her work has been broadcast on BBC radio and been published by many of the literary journals including *New Welsh Review*, *Poetry Wales*, *Iron*, *The Rialto* and *Stand*. She won Fourth Prize in the Cardiff International Poetry Competition, 2000. She is currently a part-time tutor in creative writing for Kent Adult Education.

Dan Rhodes's first book, the collection of ultra-short stories *Anthropology*, was published by Fourth Estate in 2000. After graduating from the University of Glamorgan, he went on to complete the MA in Creative Writing there. He has now left his job in the stockroom of a bookshop and is writing full time. His second book of stories, *Don't Tell Me The Truth About Love*, will be published simultaneously with the paperback of *Anthropology* on St. Valentine's Day, 2001, and his first novel, *Timoleon Vieta Come Home*, will follow. Rights to his books have already been sold in Holland, Italy, Israel and America. He lives in Kent.

Sarah Salway is a freelance journalist based in Edinburgh. Her fiction has appeared in *Shorts*, the Macallan / *Scotland on Sunday* Scottish Short Story Collection, various magazines and on the Internet. She has been shortlisted for a number of short-story competitions and is currently writing a themed collection of extracts and stories.

Victor Tapner was born in Watford and grew up in Bedfordshire. His poetry has appeared in magazines and a booklet collection *The Icarus Leaf* (Outposts Publications). He has also written a novel *Cold Rain* (Grafton Books). The poem 'Coffee Shop' was a prizewinner in the 1998 Dulwich Festival Competition and 'Thames Idol' was highly commended in the Blue Nose Poets Millennial Competition. He works as a journalist on the *Financial Times*. He lives in Essex.

Caryl Ward was a native of Pencoed, but lived also in England and America. Her first collection of poetry *Muddy Eyes* was published by Red Sharks Press and she had numerous poems and stories in magazines. She received a Welsh Arts Council New Writers' Bursary and was a prizewinner in the 1999 Rhys Davies Competition. Sadly Caryl died in July 2000, shortly before this anthology went to press.

Rob Middlehurst is from Liverpool but lived and worked in Lancaster, Bahrain and Kuwait before moving to South Wales in 1987. He is Subject Leader in Creative Writing at the University of Glamorgan. His interests include the short story, narrative and the teaching of Creative Writing. He is completing research papers on 'The Creative Writing Journal' and 'Perspectives on Narrative'. A Bridport prizewinner (short story) in 1992, he has also published work on discourse analysis.